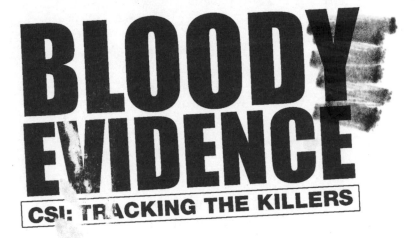

BLOODY EVIDENCE
CSI: TRACKING THE KILLERS

BY

MICHAEL SHERIDAN

First published in 2006 by

Mentor Books
43 Furze Road,
Sandyford Industrial Estate,
Dublin 18.
Republic of Ireland

Tel. +353 1 295 2112/3   Fax. +353 1 295 2114
e-mail: admin@mentorbooks.ie
www.mentorbooks.ie

A catalogue record for this book is available
from the British Library

ISBN 10: 1-84210-297-4
ISBN 13: 978-1-84210-297-8

Cover by Graham Thew
Typesetting, editing, design
and layout by Mentor Books

Printed in Ireland by ColourBooks

CONTENTS

To the forensic experts
and crime scene investigators
who make sure that victims are never silent
even in the grave.

ACKNOWLEDGMENTS

Influences and help in the writing of this and other crime books are far wider than anyone could imagine, and these can be both positive and negative. In the latter category the huge increase in crime in this country has created increased public interest in the workings of crime and the methods adopted to bring criminals, particularly killers, to justice.

One area of interest is in crime scene investigation, one of the most important tools that the forces of law employ in tracking and catching killers and I have tried to respond to that interest by dealing with some of the main disciplines that are employed by detectives and technical and medical personnel, as well as by looking at the dark art of murder.

I am always grateful for the influence of retired Detective Inspector Gerry O'Carroll, and the invaluable help along this journey of pathologist Dr Declan Gilsenan, Tara King and Lindsey Power in research, and *Irish Independent* journalist Ralph Riegel. Thanks to John Kavanagh and his wife Anne for introducing me to the Black Dahlia story.

And of course all at Mentor without whom this book would never have been completed: publisher Danny McCarthy, designer Kathryn O'Sullivan, Nicola Sedgwick in marketing, and Una Whelan, an editor who is impossible to row with and equally difficult to disagree with.

Finally Ger, Cian and Fionn who have to put up with the moody and intolerant author.

1

CRIME SCENE INVESTIGATION

'Wherever he steps, whatever he touches, even unconsciously, will serve as a silent witness against him. Not only his fingerprints, or his footprints, but his hair, the fibres from his clothing, the glass he breaks, the tool marks he leaves, the paint he scratches, the blood or semen he deposits or collects. All of these bear mute witness against him. This is evidence that does not forget. It is not confused by the excitement of the moment. It is not absent because human witnesses are. It is factual evidence. Physical evidence cannot be wrong. It cannot perjure itself; it cannot be wholly absent, only interpretation can err. Only human failure to find it, study and understand it, can diminish its value.'

Paul L. Kirk 1974

Eight-year-old Sarah Payne went missing on July 1, 2000, while visiting her grandparents in Kingston Gorse in Sussex, England. A massive search began under close media scrutiny and Sussex police investigators asked for help from the Forensic Science Service (FSS).

It wasn't long before a local man on the sex offenders'

register, Roy Whiting, became a suspect but the investigators had no evidence that he was involved. They brought him in for questioning.

Sixteen days after her disappearance Sarah's decomposing body was found in a shallow grave.

Shortly after Sarah had disappeared, her brother Lee noticed a white transit van passing along the lane. Roy Whiting had bought a white Fiat Ducato van a week before the disappearance. When police seized it, they removed all the contents which included a red sweatshirt, a pair of socks, a check shirt, a clown-patterned curtain and a petrol receipt that showed Whiting had been only a few miles from where Sarah's body was found.

A total of more than 500 items were submitted for forensic analysis and over twenty experts employed during the investigation, covering the specialities of entomology (the study of insects), pathology, geology, archaeology, environmental profiling and oil/lubricant analysis. The investigation involved one thousand personnel and cost £2 million.

When Sarah's body was discovered, it was so badly decomposed that it made identification difficult. A DNA profile was obtained from her muscle and matched to a milk tooth saved by Sarah's mother.

The only piece of Sarah's clothing to be found was a black shoe with a Velcro strap which had trapped 350 fibres. Evidence that it was in fact her shoe came from blue polyester and cotton fibres found on it which matched her school sweatshirt. The fibres were removed one by one under a low-power microscope with a pair of fine forceps and retained under sellotape.

Later, when a scientist was looking at the tapings from the red sweatshirt and the clown curtain retrieved from Whiting's van, she realised that the constituent sweatshirt fibres were unusually dark red and that they shed very easily. She then examined the fibres which had been picked off the Velcro of the shoe and saw four dark red fibres. After mounting a sample from the sweatshirt and comparing them under a high-powered microscope, a match was made, thus establishing the first tangible evidence that the murdered girl was linked to the van.

After finding these matching fibres, all the fair hair from the curtain and the sweatshirt were sent for DNA testing. From forty hairs found just one matched a hair from Sarah's head. Another link between the girl and the van had been established.

The red sweatshirt found on the front seat of Whiting's van was taped for fibres and hairs and screened for body fluids (blood, semen and saliva). The tapings taken from the sweatshirt were examined for blue fibres of the type (it was speculated) Sarah's missing dress was made of. All the fair hairs from the tapings were prepared for DNA. The collar and the cuffs were tested and provided a full profile of Whiting.

An appeal was made on the popular television programme *Crimewatch UK* for sources of the clown material found in the van. It was unusual in that it was manufactured in four colours. There were only 1,500 metres in this particular colour which had been used by Boots for curtains for branches that had baby changing rooms. Although there were other samples of clown-patterned material, none of them matched.

The fibres were teased out to mount on slides. A single multi-coloured cotton fibre on the shoe was found to match the clown curtain. The case was slowly but surely being built up and each new match connected the victim to the killer.

Two balls of Sarah's hair were retrieved from the burial site. A number of fibres were taken from them and from the body bag in which her body was placed after examination at the scene. From one of them, fibres were matched with the red sweatshirt and a pair of Whiting's socks. In the second clump, there were fibres matching the sweatshirt, socks and one fibre collected from the passenger seat of the van. One sock fibre and a fibre from the driver's seat of the van were also found in the body bag.

During the investigation a number of blue polyester fibres were found on several items. Although a source was never found to give a 'control fibre', it is thought they may have come from Sarah's dress. Sarah's friend had the same dress she was wearing the day she went missing, but in green. Examination of fibres from the green dress showed similarities to the blue polyester cotton fibres.

A total of twenty-five patchy blue polyester fibres were found on Sarah's silver jacket, known to have been worn over the missing dress and these matched nine fibres found on the red sweatshirt. Similar fibres were found in one of the hair masses, the body bag and in the pocket of Whiting's jeans. Three textured blue polyester fibres were found on the sweatshirt, matching a similar number in Sarah's hair. A few examples of a third fibre type, light blue polyester, were also found on both the sweatshirt and the hair.

Between December 2000 and November the following year an FSS team carried out 461 microspectrophotometry tests, 23 infrared spectroscopy tests and 128 thin layer chromatography tests.

During the trial the defence barrister tried to discredit the forensic evidence in a number of ways. She claimed the sweatshirt had been contaminated during its first examination. Two hairbrushes taken from the Payne family home had been sent to the lab. A scene-of-the-crime officer had put them in a tube and then in a bag on the floor. Although the seal was intact, some of the orange adhesive was exposed and human and animal hairs from the Payne's carpet were found stuck to it.

During cross examination the defence argued that, as a result of this, a 23 cm hair belonging to Sarah had first transferred onto the bag containing the sweatshirt and then to the sweatshirt itself when it was taken out of the bag for first examination. However, this examination had been completed before the hairbrushes were taken out of the exhibits store and no orange adhesive had been found in Sarah's hair when tested. Giving evidence in court, an FSS scientist told the jury it was unlikely that contamination had occurred in the manner suggested.

The defence argued that the fibres evidence wasn't important. They said that there were few fibres and that the tests were not as discriminating as DNA tests. The police scientist pointed out that, although each fibre type on its own may not be rare, taken together the combination of fibres could provide extremely strong evidence.

In December 2001 Roy Whiting was found guilty by the jury and sentenced to life imprisonment. Trial judge Mr Richard Curtis said that it was a rare case where he would recommend that life should mean life.

The discovery of a murder scene is often an accidental event by an unsuspecting member of the public even though the killing and disposal of the body may have been part of a deliberate design. Death in its most unnatural state, as is murder, is not a pretty sight, and what is a routine sight for the murder investigator or the pathologist is shocking and disturbing for anyone who encounters by chance the aftermath.

But for crime scene investigators the state of the body, the extent and pattern of injuries to head, torso and limbs, the pattern of blood spattering and smearing, or the presence and distribution of fibres can provide vital clues that may lead to the arrest and punishment of the killer.

The most important aspect of evidence collection and preservation is protecting the crime scene. This is to keep pertinent evidence uncontaminated until it can be recorded and collected. The successful prosecution of a case can hinge on the state of physical evidence at the time it is collected.

The protection of the scene begins with the arrival of the first police officer or officers and ends only when the scene is released from police control. Once the scene has been established and stabilised, it and any other adjoining areas (driveways, surrounding yards, pathways) should be roped off to prevent unauthorised people from entering and contaminating evidence.

Modern crime scene management has a three-tier perimeter. The outer perimeter is established as a border larger than the actual scene to keep onlookers and non-essential personnel away from the scene, an inner perimeter allowing for a command post and comfort area just outside the scene, and the core or the immediate scene itself.

As well as physical security of the site, it is important to protect the scene from weather and temperature changes. A tent can keep out rain, sleet, wind and snow. If the crime has been committed in a house, heating controls, windows open or closed and electrical devices should be left as originally found. Climatic conditions can have a huge bearing on the preservation of evidence. For example in freezing temperatures semen samples deteriorate much more slowly in the body of a rape and murder victim than in normal or high temperatures.

Sometimes, the arrival of additional personnel can cause problems in preserving the scene but tight control with one entrance established with one officer in charge of access can minimise the danger of unauthorised people appearing on the scene.

It is natural enough for people to gather to look at a scene where something dramatic has occurred. The officers in charge of the scene should use tact and courtesy when dealing with witnesses and crowds. This approach serves several purposes. It will encourage cooperation and may result in a witness coming forward with valuable information. Also, there is a well-known phenomenon in which the killer returns to the scene of the crime and engages the attention of investigating officers, either wittingly or unwittingly, which is another good reason not to disperse the onlooking crowd. Visual barricades such as tents can be used to prevent the victims being photographed by intrusive media.

The purpose of crime scene investigation is to establish what exactly happened to the victim and, through the collection of evidence, identify and convict the killer. This aim is pursued by carefully documenting the conditions at the crime scene and collecting and recognising all relevant physical evidence.

The investigators and technical experts who preserve and examine the crime scene play a critical and pivotal role in the investigation. Their efficiency can solve a case but their mistakes can allow the killer to walk free from a court. Like contracts, the crime scene is all about the small detail, some of it outside the range of the human eye.

Fingerprints on hard surfaces such as metal and glass are

quite visible but on softer surfaces, such as paper, they are more difficult to detect. Print powders help to make them more obvious just as the chemical luminol brings blood stains, invisible to the eye, into stark and dramatic relief. Soft-tissue X-rays can even reveal prints on flesh, a feat once believed impossible by print-gathering experts.

Television and film portrayal of the process is often inaccurate and overly dramatic. In reality crime scene investigation is difficult, painstaking and time-consuming. It is a question of no tiny stone being left unturned and every action being carefully planned and executed.

There are criminalists, document examiners, evidence custodians, firearms specialists and forensic laboratory technicians, all of whom come under the large umbrella of crime scene investigation. There are a lot of specialists involved in the process but not one that can cover all.

Evidence gathered at the scene can be split into two categories. Testimonial evidence is any witnessed account of the incident, or sight or discovery of the location. Physical evidence refers to any material items that are present. These items can be presented to prove or disprove the facts of the case. Evidence collected at a scene can:

- prove that a crime has been committed.
- establish the key elements of the crime.
- link a suspect with the scene or victim.
- establish the identity of a victim or suspect.
- corroborate verbal witness testimony.
- exonerate the innocent.

The main types of evidence that investigators deal with are:

- impressions, which include fingerprints, tool marks, footwear, fabric impressions, tyre marks and bite marks.
- forensic biology, which includes blood, semen, body fluids, hair, nail scrapings, blood-stain patterns.
- trace evidence, including gunshot residue, arson accelerant, paint, glass, fibres.
- firearms, which include weapons, gunpowder patterns, casings, projectiles, fragments, pellets, wadding and cartridges.
- questionnaires given to the public by the police.

Since most investigations start with limited information, care and common sense are necessary to minimise the chances of destroying evidence. A plan of operation is developed and put in place from the initial sweep of the scene. The objective is to decide what evidence is present, what evidence is fragile and needs to be collected as a priority, as well as what resources, equipment and assistance are necessary.

In the documentation stage, all functions should correspond and be consistent in depicting the scene. The final result of a well-documented scene is the ability of others to take the finished work and reconstruct the crime both for the clarity and accuracy of the investigation and for courtroom presentation. This stage consists of three straightforward processes: written notes and reports, photographs and sketches.

The reports are chronological and should not include

opinion or interpretation but stick to the facts. Detailed observations translated into notes are taken of everything on and in the area of the body and its relationship to furniture, doors and windows. Measurements are then made of the location, the width and height of doors, tables, beds and any other items to accurately locate the geographical area of the victim's body and evidence on the scene.

The photographs are taken as soon as possible to depict the scene as it is observed before anything is handled or moved during the examination and collection of evidence. The photographs provide a permanent visual record of the crime scene, position of the body, injuries sustained and items of evidence collected from the scene.

The forensic photographer has a huge variety of equipment to deal with different factors affecting the scene but basically uses the three camera positions familiar to the celluloid world – master shots showing overall views of the scene; medium shots showing the relationship of items; and close-ups of the evidence at the scene. All stationary evidence where the photograph will be used to assist in the analytical process are taken on a tripod, with proper lighting techniques applied. A second shot adding a measuring device is also utilised.

Overall photos of the scene are taken to show the approach to the area, street signs, street-light locations in relation to the actual scene, street addresses and identifying objects at the scene. In a house, pictures are taken of every room even though there is no apparent connection with the scene.

Detailed photographs are taken of the body and its immediate vicinity and the general location and items and objects within it. A boom is sometimes operated to take pictures from ceiling height. This perspective can reveal the presence of objects missed when viewed from eye and ground level.

Spectators watching the activities are also photographed in case the perpetrator has returned to the scene to watch police at work. These photographs may also help identify reluctant witnesses.

Sketches are widely used along with reports and photographs to document the scene. A crime scene sketch is simply a drawing that accurately shows the appearance of the scene. The sketch is drawn to show items and their position and relationship. While it is not an architectural drawing made to scale, it does include exact measurements when required. The advantage of a sketch is that it can cover a large area and be drawn to leave out clutter that might appear in photographs. Also, photographs can sometimes give a distorted view of the relationship of the body to other fixed objects due to camera angle, size of lens and lighting. It is then possible to use the diagram in conjunction with photos to give a more accurate depiction of the scene.

Care and method are at the basis of all crime scene investigations, and particular caution is exercised in approaching the body of the victim to make sure not to disturb or contaminate any evidence in the immediate surroundings.

In 1994 the bungling activities of LAPD investigators at the crime scene of the murders of Nicole Brown Simpson, estranged wife of famous football player and movie star OJ Simpson, and her boyfriend Ronald Goldman, resulted in the contamination of vital evidence. Lack of proper protection led to the presence of bloody shoeprints all over the scene, which turned out to be those of responding officers. Contaminating the crime scene to such a degree caused trace evidence to be disturbed and moved.

Blood evidence, which would have solved the case beyond any reasonable doubt, also disappeared. A crime scene photograph shows Nicole lying face downwards, her long, silky hair falling down to a ground saturated with the blood from her slashed throat. She seems to be leaning forward, the halter from her dress stretching across the back of her neck. There are a dozen or more droplets of blood spread across her upper back. Her position and the fact that the body had not been moved at the time the photograph was taken, meant that the blood on her back could not have been hers, or indeed that of the other victim, her boyfriend Ronald Goldman. It had to belong to the killer who clearly sustained a wound in the savage attack. Inexplicably, no swab of that blood was taken for DNA analysis at the scene or, even more bizarrely, when the body was taken to the mortuary two hours later. The body was washed down, destroying the most vital evidence in the case. OJ Simpson had a deep cut on one of his hands.

An investigator has to be careful not to jump to an

immediate conclusion about what has happened or posit an early theory which might be hard to dislodge. It is better to generate several theories, retaining those which are not eliminated by new information coming to light. Reasonable inferences about what happened are produced from scene appearance and information from witnesses. These will help guide the investigator to document specific conditions and recognise valuable evidence. The investigators make a close visual examination of the body and the area immediately around it. They look for physical clues such as defence wounds on the arms, foreign material under the fingernails, bullet exit and entry wounds. The investigating eye notes what clothes are on the corpse or what clothing is missing and whether folds or rolls indicate that the body has been dragged from another position.

After the photographer has finished his work the focus returns to the victim. By then the pathologist has arrived to conduct a preliminary examination before the body is eventually removed to a mortuary for a full postmortem. The medical investigator notes whether the eyes are opened or closed, the colour of the skin, nails, hands and lips, and the presence or absence of blood, saliva or vomit.

The body of the victim is a crime scene in itself and provides a wealth of information for investigators of a murder or killing. The classic principle of exchange discovered by the father of forensic science Dr Edmund Locard is that when two people come in contact, particularly in a violent struggle, fibres, hair, blood, semen and other properties are interchanged, leaving evidence on the body of a murder victim which can be directly linked to the killer.

Injuries to the body are examined and the presence of cuts, bruises, stab wounds or bullet wounds is noted. The temperature of the body is taken and the extent of rigor mortis is used to establish an approximate time of death. The temperature of the surroundings is taken to compare with the body temperature.

When the pathologist has completed the on-scene examination, the body is removed to the mortuary and further examination of the scene and evidence collection is continued.

Once investigators and the pathologist have completed their preliminary examination and the body has been removed, the team then move on to systematically check the remainder of the house, business, vehicle or location and carefully note items of evidence or conditions which may shed extra light on the investigation.

They can include:

Doors: Are they locked or bolted (from inside or outside)? Are there marks of forced entry? Does the doorbell work? Is there a door knocker? Are there scratches around the keyhole?

Windows: Are they locked or unlocked, open or broken? The type and position of curtains, drapes or blinds are noted.

Newspapers and mail: Is the mail unopened or read? Postmarks on the envelopes and dates on the newspapers are checked.

Lights: Which lights were on when the crime was discovered? How are they controlled – by timers, motion sensors or switches? Can they be seen from the outside? Are the bulbs broken or unscrewed?

Smells: Did the first investigating officer on the scene notice any distinctive smells such as alcohol, tobacco, gas, perfume, gunpowder or any other unusual odours?

Kitchen: Was food being prepared? If so, what kind? The food may or may not correspond with the contents of the victim's stomach. Are there signs of attempting to destroy evidence, such as burning or washing?

Heating or air conditioning: What heating system is it? Is the place ventilated or not? The thermostat setting should be checked.

Signs of entertainment should be checked, such as empty bottles, cups, glasses, all fertile ground for evidence.

Contents of ashtrays, cigarette packs and butts: If present, it is vital that they be properly preserved, as DNA can be extracted.

Contents of bins and waste baskets should be thoroughly checked.

Clocks, microwave and DVD settings need examination and checking.

Bathrooms: Towels should be checked for evidence such as blood. Hand basins and bath drains should be examined for hair, fibre or blood evidence. The perpetrator could have taken a shower or bath. The toilet and cabinets also need checking.

Disorder: Are there signs of a struggle in any of the rooms?

In shootings, how many bullets were fired? Cartridge cases must be collected and bullet holes located and numbered. These items should be photographed, marked and identified with numbered markers to prevent them being moved, altered or damaged.

Stabbings or beatings: Are there weapons present and were they already at the location (weapons of opportunity) or brought from outside?

Blood: Characteristics such as the degree of coagulation, type, pooling, spots, stains, smears or spatters are noted. Blood-spatter analysis helps to reconstruct the crime in a minute and highly accurate fashion.

Hangings and strangulation: What instrument or means was used? Was it obtained in the house or brought to the scene? The victim should never be cut down, if obviously dead, until a proper examination is completed. Even an apparent suicide is suspicious until proved otherwise; it could have been staged.

Stairs, hallways, entrances and exits to the scene must be checked for footprints, debris, discarded items and fingerprints.

A check is made for items that should not be at the location naturally, such as mud, leaves, sand, grass. A perpetrator may bring such items from outside the location on shoes or clothes and unknowingly provide vital evidence.

Ransacking: What items are missing and may have been taken away by the perpetrator?

Bloody Evidence

Possible hiding places for weapons: If panicked, a perpetrator may try to conceal the weapon quickly.

Personal information: Is the victim married or in a relationship? As much should be established about the relationship as possible. Was there a history of abuse, infidelity, alcohol or drug abuse, monetary problems or an impending split or divorce? A partner can be the prime suspect and such information can quickly establish if there was a pressing motive for killing.

The painstaking gathering of evidence at a crime scene, the careful observation and recording of details, is vital to an investigation.

2

BLOOD TYPING AND DNA

Forensic evidence has come a long way since Sherlock
Holmes, the original scientific detective who made his first
entrance to the world of detection in the pages of *A Study in
Scarlet*. He was in a laboratory holding a test tube and adding
chemicals to a tiny amount of blood diluted in a litre of water.

> A few white crystals and then . . . some drops of
> transparent fluid . . . In an instant the contents
> assumed a dull mahogany colour, and a
> brownish dust was precipitated to the bottom of
> the glass jar.
>
> 'I've found it, I've found it,' he shouted to my
> companion, running towards us with a test tube
> in his hand. 'I have found a reagent which is
> precipitated by haemoglobin and by nothing
> else. Why man, it is the most practical medico-
> legal discovery for years. Don't you see that it
> gives us an infallible test for blood stains?'

This was 1887 and it would take over a decade to invent a
specific test for human blood and a few more years to hone

the test to identify the blood of any animal – a clear case of fiction pre-dating fact. At that time, there was no way to determine whether a dried blood stain was human or animal.

Holmes was responsible for another truism when remarking on the phrase that genius is an infinite capacity for taking pains. 'It is a bad definition,' he said, 'but it does apply to detective work.' And that applies to this day, despite all the advances in forensic science. Footwork and sheer, hard slog will always be a major factor in the art of detection as the Sarah Payne and many other cases prove.

In 1900 Paul Uhlenhuth found a method of determining the origin of unknown blood using a precipitating antiserum. Realising the forensic potential of his discovery he produced a range of serums from different animals from which blood could be tested. He tried his method on blood stains of different ages and discovered individual antibodies (proteins produced in the blood which destroy bacteria) could identify the individual animals. The method was also applicable to humans. Killers could now be targeted by blood.

His work was welcomed by criminologists who developed practices that would become standard in every forensic laboratory in the world. As in much science practice, there was a simultaneous discovery going on elsewhere by an equally brilliant man. His name was Dr Karl Landsteiner and he was based in Vienna.

Landsteiner wanted to find out why so many blood transfusions resulted in blood clots and death, suspecting that blood contains properties that are not universally shared. He devised an experiment mixing together human blood cells and serum. His conclusion was that blood could be broken down into four groups – A, B, AB and O and that a person's blood group could be determined by adding a small amount of known antibody to a blood sample. Depending on the antibody added, the blood cells would clump together, thus identifying the blood group.

Landsteiner's work earned him a Nobel Prize many years later. It was now possible to give a blood transfusion without the danger of serious clotting and his work also led to the discovery that blood groups are inherited. It opened the door to blood-typing in the forensic field and, ultimately, DNA fingerprinting.

Outside the grind of science and the laboratory it took a domestic situation to push it on to a new level. A suspicious Italian wife of all things.

On September 7, 1915, a small man walked into the Institute of Forensic Medicine at the University of Turin and asked to see Dr Leon Lattes. He wore his best suit and carried a package wrapped in newspaper and tied with string. The doctor was in the lab where he spent most of his day working on blood groupings. His visitor was Renzo Girardi, a construction worker.

He gave the package to the scientist and it contained a white shirt with two brownish stains on the tails. He then told his story. Three months before, he had visited friends in his home village outside Turin and ended up in a tavern drinking to a late hour. When he returned home his jealous wife accused him of infidelity, though he protested his innocence. He eventually fell asleep in his clothes. The next morning he took off his white shirt and saw two stains on it. He had not a clue where they had come from but his wife was convinced that they were the blood stains of another woman.

Girardi told the doctor that he had no money but he implored him to prove that the stains did not come from a woman. Lattes's first task was to discover the blood group of the dried stains. Firstly, he had to carefully restore the blood to its original liquid state. He cut the fabric around the stain and dropped it into a test tube containing the appropriate concentration of saline solution. The next morning, Lattes was able to remove the tiny piece of cloth from the now dark solution.

He ran a test that showed the blood was human. Further tests identified the blood group as A, which matched Girardi's. It transpired he suffered from prostrate problems which proved to be the source of the staining. The doctor was not only satisfied by the results of his painstaking tests but also that peace had been restored to the family.

The science of serology, as such work became known, was introduced into more and more criminal cases. The field was just being narrowed down, however. Scientists still could not tell whether a blood stain came from one particular person, because the blood groupings were far too large.

In 1925 Landsteiner and a Japanese team simultaneously discovered that the same antigens (toxins which cause the body to produce antibodies) found in blood are secreted into other bodily fluids – semen, saliva, tears and sweat – by 80% of the population. This meant that not only could a murderer be tracked down by his blood but a rapist could be identified by his semen. Forensic detection had taken another big leap forward.

However, while blood-typing provided good circumstantial evidence when added to other strands of evidence, it was not going to convict a killer on its own. It would take just over a quarter of a century for this to happen.

The human body is composed of 100 trillion cells which make up every organ and part of the body. Under a powerful microscope, it can be seen that cells contain a small dark shape known as a nucleus, the centre of growth and development. Inside the nucleus there are twenty-three pairs of short ribbons which German biologist Walther Fleming named chromosomes. Genes – small sections of chromosomes – are responsible for the transmission of hereditary characteristics.

In the late nineteenth century Swiss scientist Johann Miescher had discovered that the chromosomes in each cell nucleus were composed of more than protein. He subjected the chromosomes to intense microscopic study. The short ribbons, he established, were composed of a mixture of protein and acid, which he named nuclein.

With further experiments he managed to extract a pure acid, to which a pupil of his later gave the name deoxyribonucleic acid – DNA. The scientist would have made a major discovery had he established the function of DNA, but he died of tuberculosis at the age of fifty-one in 1895. In the years that followed, scientists were focusing on proteins, and DNA was neglected.

In the early 1950s two young scientists at Cambridge took on the case. American James Watson and Englishman Francis Crick dreamed of solving the enigma of the structure of DNA. Watson and Crick set about building a model of a DNA molecule, working on a set of molecular models resembling the toys of pre-school children. The pair began to play. Their blocks were the four nitrogen-containing bases of DNA: adenine – A, guanine – G, thymine – T and cytosine – C, which they thought would be linked with a sugar phosphate backbone.

Watson, using data which said that there was the same amount of A and T in each DNA molecule and similarly an equal proportion of C and G, constructed a model that paired them together in a double spiral or helix.

The DNA was like a spiral staircase: the rungs were the AT and CG pairs, the banisters were sugar phosphate chains.

If the bonds were broken in two, the ladder would peel apart and the bases attach to a new partner. In this way DNA could copy itself infinitely using the chemical affinities between the paired letters. Watson and Crick had discovered the secret of life.

Not obvious then in 1953 but, in time, it would have just as great an impact on another discipline – the art of forensic detection. That would take another thirty-three years.

Refrigerated red blood cells have a shelf life of about forty-two days, while serum containing white blood cells can last under refrigeration for up to a year. DNA can be extracted from blood and from sperm, bone marrow, tooth pulp and hair roots.

To test for DNA, blood samples are collected from the victim, defendant, and crime scene. White blood cells are then separated from red blood cells and DNA extracted from the nuclei of white blood cells. An enzyme is used to cut fragments of the DNA strand, which are then put into a bed of gel with electrodes at either end. An electric current causes the DNA fragments to separate according to their length. An absorbent blotter soaks up the imprint. It is radioactively treated, and an X-ray photograph is produced.

The result is that the DNA pattern in the photograph is completely individual and cannot be attributed to anyone else. The odds against the identity being wrong or mistaken are in the billions to one bracket. The killer may lie but DNA never does.

3
TIME OF DEATH

In many fictional accounts, in print, on television and on celluloid, time of death is portrayed as an exact science but according to Assistant State Pathologist Declan Gilsenan who has worked on many Irish murder cases, there are no reliable methods which can guarantee one hundred percent accuracy. The following is his assessment of the problems and provides an insight into the nature of the bodily changes that occur in the aftermath of death.

> The only sure way to pinpoint the time of a homicidal death is with a witness or by a confession. Slotting a suspect between alibis may be grist to the mill of Miss Marple, Hercules Poirot, Jessica Fletcher and friends but the real world is not like that. Happily, time of death is not important or contentious in the majority of homicide cases. This is just as well because our best methods are sadly inaccurate and despite the application of more and more sophisticated scientific methods and equipment we have not made any significant advances to increase the accuracy of the time of death

estimation over the past fifty years.

Death is, primarily, a cessation of bodily functions, such as breathing, circulation of the blood and biochemical activity, the last two of which give rise to observable phenomena. The end of circulation quickly leads to the sedimentation of blood to the lowest part of the body. For a body lying on its back, it is to the back of the body. For a body lying on its left side it is to the left side. Because the weight of the body compresses those parts in firm contact with the surfaces, there are pale areas at these points.

A hanging or suspended body develops hypostasis [pooling of blood] in the lower limbs, lower body and lower areas of the upper limbs. This usually appears about half an hour after death and is at its maximum ten to twelve hours later. There is considerable variability with this occurrence which makes it of little use in determining the time of death.

Following death, the muscles of the body are usually soft and limp for a period of between three and six hours. Then, the muscles stiffen, most noticeably in the smaller muscles, jaw and neck, gradually extending to the larger groups of muscles of the body.

Rigor mortis, as this process is known, is usually

at its maximum six to twelve hours after death. Rigor mortis continues for twenty to forty hours and then begins to recede.

The onset, duration and degree of rigor mortis is influenced by the size and muscularity of the body, by various medical conditions and the temperature of the surroundings. These variables make rigor mortis a completely inaccurate means of measuring the postmortem interval.

Algor mortis, or postmortem cooling, still represents the most accurate method of estimating the postmortem interval in the first forty hours. Most methods assume that the body is at the normal temperature of 37°C at the moment of death but this may not always be the case. If the person dies in freezing conditions or is suffering from a high fever before death, the starting temperature can be seriously altered.

Body cooling is not linear but displays variation in the two to three hours after death. Cooling then occurs at an average of 1°C per hour. Factors such as clothing, air movement around the body and air temperature all influence the result and often in a manner that is not easily predictable.

The temperature of the body is established by inserting a thermometer in the rectum or into the liver through the abdominal wall.

As an example of confounding factors, I once encountered a case in which the deceased was killed while immersed in a warm bath and then wrapped in a sleeping bag, ready for disposal. The temperature of the body was in excess of the normal 37°C some hours after death.

Bodies immersed in cold water do not follow the above rules due to direct conduction of the heat away from the body into the water.

More complex methods have been employed to take account of the variable factors but with limited success, because the conditions vary so much.

Postmortem putrefaction or rotting usually begins after three days with greenish discoloration of the lower wall of the abdomen. This purplish-green colour spreads gradually over the body, producing a marbling effect. Gas is formed in the tissues and causes swelling of the neck and face and bloating of the stomach. Foul-smelling fluid comes out of the body and any wounds present.

In the unusual circumstance where there is no blowfly [maggot] infestation, the tissues darken and dry, leading eventually to mummification. The variables that affect the rate of rotting may include the surrounding heat, moisture and, most significantly, the presence of septicaemia [blood poisoning] in the deceased before death. I have seen a body eight hours after death with septicaemia present, displaying an appearance more appropriate to a body eight days after death.

Blowfly infestation is more common in summer but less likely in the winter months when the temperature stays below 12°C. The science of forensic entomology is the study of the effects of insects on the dead body. It is a useful tool in the estimation of the time of death over the period of days to weeks. By recognising the stages of maturation of the insect life present on the body and making due allowance for the effect of the surrounding temperature, the forensic entomologist can make a useful contribution to the estimation of the time since death.

Dr Gilsenan's assessment is supported by all up-to-date research in the area but it is useful to examine further the whole area of time of death and the physiological changes which happen in the aftermath of what Shakespeare describes as 'the shuffling off of the mortal coil'. Research in forensic science on the subject from the University of Dundee is illuminating.

Establishing the times of assault and death has a direct bearing on the legal questions of alibi and opportunity. If the suspect is able to prove he was elsewhere when the fatal injury was inflicted then he has an alibi and his innocence is implicit. Conversely, if the time of lethal assault coincides with the time when the suspect was known to be in the vicinity of the victim, then the suspect had the opportunity to commit the crime.

With bodies recovered from fires, it is critical to establish whether death occurred before or during the fire. Similarly, if a body is recovered from water, a critical question is whether the victim was alive or dead when they entered the water.

In Britain and Ireland the degree of decomposition after twenty-four hours in the height of summer may be the equivalent of ten to fourteen days in the depths of winter. Cold weather has had the effect of preserving DNA evidence, such as semen in a rape and murder case, long beyond the time it takes to deteriorate under warm conditions. This has resulted in the trapping of killers who were convinced that evidence they left would never be matched to them.

After normal burial, the rate at which the body decomposes will depend to a large extent on the depth of the grave, the warmth of the soil, the efficiency of the drainage and the durability of the coffin. The restriction of air in deep burials, particularly in clay soil, will retard decomposition, but never prevent it altogether.

Buried in well-drained soil, an adult body is reduced to a skeleton in about ten years and a child's body in about five years. It is generally accepted that in the first forty-eight hours after death, changes are due to organisms already present in the body. According to an old rule of thumb, one week of putrefaction in air is equivalent to two weeks in water, which is equivalent to eight weeks buried in soil, given the same environmental temperature.

As outlined by Dr Gilsenan, the first signs of decomposition is marbling of the skin and the formation of putrid gas, causing the body to swell. The greenish-purple face appears bloated with the eyelids swollen and tightly closed, the lips swollen and pouting, the cheeks puffed out and the distended tongue protruding from the mouth.

Head hair and other body hair becomes loose at the roots and can be easily pulled out in large clumps. The finger- and toenails become detached, often with large sheets of skin. The neck, trunk and limbs become massively swollen, giving the false impression of gross obesity. Finally, the putrid gases, which are under considerable pressure, find an escape and the whole mass of decomposing soft tissues collapses.

The putrefactive changes which have taken place until this time are relatively rapid when contrasted to the terminal decay of the body. When the internal juices have been drained away and the soft tissues have shrunk, the speed of decay is much reduced.

The next stage, adipocere, is characterised by the transformation of fatty tissues into a yellowish-white substance with a sweet, rancid odour. The medico-legal importance of this condition lies not in establishing the time of death, but rather in its ability to preserve the body to an extent which can aid in personal identification and the recognition of injuries. The presence of adipocere indicates that the postmortem interval is at least weeks and probably several months.

Mummification is the next stage and involves the dehydration of the tissues. The body shrivels and is converted into a leathery or parchment-like mass of skin and tendons surrounding the bone. The internal organs are often decomposed but may be preserved. This stage develops in conditions of dry heat. The forensic importance of mummification also lies in the preservation of tissue which aids in personal identification and recognition of injuries. The time required for the mummification of a body cannot be precisely stated, but in ideal conditions could be well advanced by the end of a few weeks.

Dr Gilsenan states that all methods used to determine time of death have wide margins of error and, while undoubtedly useful to point investigators in the right direction, should be used with extreme caution as evidence in a court of law.

4

FINGERPRINTS

Identification of criminals up to the late nineteenth century relied on the visual which left the process wide open to personal prejudice and miscarriage of justice. It also enabled criminals to easily avoid conviction by using a disguise or false papers.

A doctor and medical missionary working in Japan in the mid-nineteenth century, Henry Faulds, realised that fingerprints could solve the problems that identification caused the British legal system. He noticed that on pieces of ancient and more modern pottery there were patterns of ridges. He deduced and confirmed that these were the impressions left by the potter's fingers. He collected prints of friends, colleagues and patients and suspected strongly from his research that each fingerprint had its own distinct and unique pattern of ridges.

He was initially reluctant to publish his findings because of the inherent danger of incorrect identification. He first determined to prove that each individual's fingerprints were unique and stayed the same all their lives. His findings were published in the prestigious scientific journal *Nature* but elicited little interest either from the scientific community or police investigators.

To further divert from his research, a young clerk named Alphonse Bertillon, working in the Prefecture of Police in Paris, was also hunting for a proper process and method of identifying criminals. Bertillon began with body measurement and eye colour. His system of measurement did not impress police investigators more attuned to hard slog, instinct and training as the route to catch criminals but his persistence paid off and eventually he was given his own department of identification with staff to help him. In 1883 he identified a criminal who until then had successfully hidden his identity. He followed up in the next year by identifying over 200 habitual criminals by the process of body measurement.

In another continent Edward Henry who worked in the office of Inspector General of the Bengal Police, assisted by Azizul Haque, ordered that, as well as body measurements, ten-digit fingerprint sets should be taken from criminals. The fingerprints were taken on a specially designed slip. Haque filed his slips in a large cabinet containing 1,200 pigeon holes. He also devised an equation for establishing a fingerprint set classification without referring to the cabinet. Within five minutes he could pull out a card that needed to be checked from any part of the cabinet. In June 1897 identification of criminals by fingerprints was adopted throughout India with Haque's classification system as its basis.

Henry returned to England and established the fingerprint branch of Scotland Yard in 1901. A year later the system was in place in many European countries as well as in New York. The next test was to have it accepted by the courts.

In 1905 an elderly couple, Thomas and Ann Farrow, were brutally murdered in a paint shop in Deptford, London. The scene was examined by famous Scotland Yard detective Melville McNaughten, an enthusiastic supporter of fingerprinting as a powerful investigative tool. But the role of fingerprinting and its credibility as evidence had never been tested in a major murder case.

At the blood-covered scene there was not much of evidential value but McNaughten found a thumbprint on an emptied cash box. It was matched to a man by the name of Alfred Stratton who had been arrested along with his brother Albert. While both Henry and McNaughten were excited, they were also apprehensive because the fingerprint evidence was the only solid evidence linking Stratton with the murder.

Eyewitness evidence placing the brothers at or near the shop proved that they had the opportunity but not that they actually carried out the killing. The motive was clearly robbery and the killings were to prevent the perpetrators from being identified by the shop owner and his wife. At the time, repeated criminal acts were given very heavy sentences by the courts.

Edward Henry secured the services of a famous prosecutor, Richard Muir, who was both admired and highly feared by his court adversaries. He had an ability to second guess defence strategy and was also a brilliant performer in court. Muir never underestimated the opposition and he knew that the case against the Strattons was not cut and dried and would hinge on the fingerprint evidence.

He urged the investigators to assemble as much circumstantial evidence as possible particularly placing the brothers near the shop at the time of the murders and establishing if they had afterwards gone on a spending spree.

Muir opened the prosecution case at the Old Bailey on May 5, 1905, describing in detail the brutal murder of paint shop manager Thomas Farrow and his wife Ann. The court was hushed as the prosecutor graphically reconstructed the horrendous final moments of the two elderly people and the wanton violence employed by the robbers whose desire for money was totally superseded by their lust for blood and the necessity to kill the only witnesses to the crime.

At the defence table Muir could see out of the corner of his eye fingerprint expert Henry Faulds. Faulds would dispute the prosecution use of the forensic evidence, believing that one fingerprint match was unreliable.

Muir set out the evidence provided by eyewitnesses who saw the Stratton brothers loitering near the shop, coming out of the shop and then later having more money than they could logically account for. He claimed that the brothers used iron jemmies to force open the door of the shop and then afterwards employed them as the murder weapons. Stocking masks had been left behind plus the thumbprint of one of the men on the cash box.

Muir then called no fewer than forty witnesses to back up his case which was that the men had the motive, opportunity and the means to carry out the crime and were placed at the scene of the murders.

Alfred's live-in girlfriend Annie Cromarty stated that shortly before the murders they had not enough money for food or fuel but afterwards he had no problem in buying supplies. Alfred had disposed of some clothes which, given their circumstances, he could ill afford to do. He had also asked her to give him an alibi for the night of and the day and night following the murders. She noted that after the murders had happened Alfred's trousers smelt of paraffin which Muir proposed had been picked up in the paint shop.

The prosecution witnesses were robustly cross-examined by the defence barristers HG Rooth appearing for Alfred and Harold Morris for Albert. As artfully as Muir constructed his case they began to pull it apart, exposing contradictions and weaknesses in the evidence given by witnesses and casting doubt on their credibility.

Rooth was sufficiently confident to put his client in the box. Alfred gave his version of what happened on the night of the murders. He said that his brother had come to the window of his lodging house in the early hours of the morning saying that he had no money for lodgings. By the time he had dressed, his brother had gone but he later met him on the street and they both returned to his lodging house and Albert slept on the floor.

Muir was down but not out and pulled an ace from his witness card – an assistant jailer in whom Albert had confided. Albert had more or less confessed to him, saying that his brother had led him into the crime and would hang while he would get ten years. While the judge ruled the statement as admissible evidence he said it could not be used against Alfred and the jury must ignore it in that context but not so in regard to Albert. Now all the prosecution had against Alfred was the thumb print.

Muir moved on and called Det Inspector Charles Collins. A blackboard was set up for him to illustrate his evidence. Collins explained fingerprinting evidence to the jury and how it could be matched up. He was a good witness, calm and collected, and did not blind the jury with science but tried to make every point as simple as possible. The conclusion of his testimony coincided with the completion of the prosecution case. An exhausted Muir sat down with the feeling that despite all his expertise and efforts, the outcome of the case hung on a knife edge.

But now the defence introduced an eminent expert to contest Collins's theory. Dr John Garson took the stand. The defence went through his qualifications for the benefit of the jury. Garson disputed almost every point of Collins's evidence. Hearing such evidence for the first time and listening to two experts contradict the importance and the credibility of the fingerprinting method was very confusing for the jury. Even if the jury accepted and believed the prosecution theory, the defence had introduced more than an element of doubt.

It was up to Muir to eliminate that. Once again this extraordinary advocate produced another ace from his pocket at the most crucial stage of the proceedings. Muir handed the eminent witness a piece of paper and asked him to read it out to the court. It was a copy of a letter that Garson had written to the Stratton lawyers offering his expertise and stating that he would not hesitate to say that the way fingerprinting was being used by the police would bring it into disrepute.

The prosecution counsel then handed Garson another piece of paper and asked him to read it to the court. It was a copy of a letter written by him to the Director of Public Prosecutions in which Garson offered to testify for the prosecution. The expert obviously did not care about the value of the evidence, he was merely selling himself to the highest bidder. Both letters were written on the same date. Muir asked him how he could justify his position. Garson answered that he was an independent witness. An untrustworthy one, the judge remarked.

In an instant the defence position on the most valuable but complex piece of evidence was blown apart. The closing arguments were made by both sides and the jury retired. Just two hours later the foreman announced the verdict: Guilty.

It is highly likely that without the fingerprint evidence the Strattons would not have been convicted. Instead, they both perished on the gallows. For the first time in a criminal trial, it was illustrated that forensic science had no opinion and no bias. Killers may say what they want but forensics speak the truth. Fingerprinting was now an essential component in the progressing art of crime scene investigation. It still remains one of the most important components.

The science of fingerprinting has of course, changed radically since that time but in essence the effect is the same. The methods of recovery and classification have advanced but are based on the same simple theory – the prints at birth are there for life; no two individuals have the exact same patterns and, when properly catalogued, prints can be retrieved, regardless of the size of the database.

The forensic print examiner uses a number of tools to lift prints including powders, brushes, lifting tape, cards, printing ink, flashlight and batteries, camera, casting and moulding supplies, rulers, compass, pencil markers and pens. Once there is a visible print to work with, the location at the scene is documented and, in most cases, photographed. The print is lifted and put on to a card for permanent storage.

Patent prints are those whose details are obvious to the naked eye. They are prints made observable by additional substances which coat the skin and are transferred to the object where the print is found. These substances could vary from a number of external sources such as oil, paint, dust, sand or sweat on the fingers or palms. Depending on the surface of the object, patent prints will need different methods of collection. If very visible, photography can be sufficient, otherwise they may need to be lifted and analysed further under laboratory conditions.

Latent prints – those not visible to the naked eye – can be raised in the right light but others need the application of powder or chemical treatment.

The third type, impressed prints, are not transfers but

actual physical mouldings of a set of friction ridges. Wax, gum or any malleable surface has the potential to contain print impressions. Blood can be a perfect substance for picking up print impressions.

Lab testing provides the means to properly evaluate the print composition and the surface on which it was found. It is not unusual for prints to receive preliminary processing at the scene and to be later treated by chemical processing in the lab.

All prints fall within one of eight patterns consisting of arches, loops and whorls. Each of the eight fingers and two thumbs generates a description and the complete code exactly describes the print so that it is uniquely identifiable and easily retrieved from a database.

While the skin on the hand feels relatively smooth, there are ridges or raised areas which allow us to handle objects without their slipping, for example turning the pages of a newspaper or book. These ridges provide further meat for the forensic examiner as each ridge has specific features for classification.

The ridges fork into separate ridges, terminate, connect and reconnect like bridges, again providing entirely individual characteristics and each set of ten prints contains differing numbers of each of these features, providing rich hunting ground for investigators and the potential for one hundred percent identification.

Fingerprints properly collected, identified and accurately compared can provide the ace card in the detection pack.

5

HAIR AND FIBRE ANALYSIS

Hair found on the head, pubic region, arms, legs and other body areas has characteristics that can determine its origin. Because hairs can be transferred during physical contact, their presence can connect a suspect to a victim or a crime scene. The types of hair found and the condition and number of hairs all provide highly valuable evidence in a criminal investigation.

Hair evidence is analysed in the laboratory with a comparison microscope which allows the examiner to compare at the same time the hair's characteristics with samples taken from a perpetrator, making it much easier to find a match.

The significance of hair examination results is dependent on the method of evidence collection used at the crime scene, the process techniques used and the experience of the person examining the hair. Head and pubic hairs are routinely held as more significant and reliable than hairs from other parts of the body.

The hair identification process involves the examination and comparison of hair characteristics along the entire length of the hair or hairs. Longer hairs have more characteristics to compare, and the greater the variation along the length, the greater the significance.

While head hair is usually the longest found on the body, it is also the most subject to change such as the use of dye, rinses and other chemical applications. It can also be affected by environmental conditions – sun, wind or frost. This makes it important for investigators to take hair samples from both suspect and victim as soon as possible.

Pubic hairs are also routinely compared in the forensic laboratory. As with head hairs considerable variation exists between individuals. Pubic hair is not subject to as much change as head hair, so samples taken up to a year after a crime can still be suitable for comparison. However it is still important to get a sample as soon after the crime as possible.

Head hair is the most suitable and reliable in determining the racial origin of the perpetrator or a victim in an advanced state of decomposition.

A victim's family, co-workers and other people who may have logical contact with or access to the victim or the crime scene should be considered for hair examination. Establishing association is hugely significant in crimes involving strangers because there is no logical connection. On the other hand, if, for example, a husband is involved in the murder of his wife, then fibre evidence is of less value to investigators. If his hairs or fibres are found on the scene and on the body, his presence on an ongoing basis would ensure that such evidence could not be an effective weapon in a prosecution case and easily challenged by a defence team in court.

Textile fibres can also be transferred during physical contact and can place a suspect at the scene of a crime. The transfer of fibres is dependent on the duration and nature of the contact between the suspect and victim. The more violent and close the contact, the greater the likelihood of this evidence being deposited. Fibres can also transfer from a carpet, bed or furniture at a crime scene.

A fibre is the smallest unit of textile material that has a length many times greater than its diameter. Fibres can occur naturally as plant and animal fibres but are also man-made. Polyester and nylon fibres are the most common man-made fibres, followed by acrylics, rayons and acetates. A fibre can be spun with other fibres to form a yarn which can be woven or knitted to form a fabric. The type and length of the fibre used, the type of spinning method, and the type of fabric construction all affect the transfer of fibres and the significance of fibre associations.

Fibre transfers can either be direct (primary) or indirect (secondary). A primary transfer occurs when a fibre is transferred from a fabric directly onto a victim's clothing, whereas a secondary transfer occurs when already transferred fibres on the clothing of a suspect transfer to the clothing of a victim.

An important consideration is the length of time lapsed between the actual physical contact and the collection of clothing items from the suspect or victim. If the victim is immobile, very little fibre loss will take place, whereas the suspect's clothing will lose transferred fibres quickly. The likelihood of finding transferred fibres on the day after the alleged contact may be remote, depending on the subsequent use or handling of that clothing. Fibres will be lost if the suspect moves about, brushes or washes the clothing. It is difficult to predict how many fibres might remain on the clothing after a given period of time, but it is important for investigators to retrieve and preserve the clothing as soon as possible.

It may be argued that the large volume of fabric produced in mass manufacturing reduces the significance of any fibre association discovered in a criminal case. It can never be stated with certainty that a fibre originated from a particular garment because other garments were produced using the same fibre, type and colour. The inability to positively associate a fibre with a particular garment to the exclusion of all other garments, however, does not mean that fibre association is without value. In many murder cases the association can prove crucial in connecting the perpetrator to the victim and, in concert with other evidence, in solving the crime.

There is the matter of apparent coincidence. When fibres that match the clothing of the suspect are found on the clothing of the victim, two conclusions may be drawn: the fibres originated from the suspect, or the fibres originated from another fabric source that not only was composed of fibres of the exact type and colour, but also was in a place where the transfer of fibres could occur through primary or secondary contact. Most unlikely as any investigator would note. Without a doubt, more evidence would be needed but such an occurrence would stretch the bounds of coincidence and logic, as the following horrendous case of serial murder proves.

The red fibre

It was a red fibre. But nobody could connect it to anything until it was too late. But even late it would be a vital clue and vital evidence.

On May 13, 1984, two teenage boys walking across a field near Tampa, Florida made a gruesome discovery: the decomposed remains of a nude woman. They ran home to their parents who immediately contacted the police.

Capt Gary Terry and Detective Lee Baker from the Hillsborough County sheriff's office arrived on the scene. They were confronted by the sight of a female body infested with maggots. She was lying face down, her wrists tied loosely behind her back and a noose draped around her neck. The detectives established from the severe bruising visible on her body that the victim had been badly beaten before death. Her hips had been crudely broken to effect a pose with her legs wide apart. It was the classical work of a sexual psychopath, an act of sadistic revenge on women who, in the killer's mind, are nothing more than whores. The detectives knew that this was the work of a very dangerous man who would more than likely strike again. They would have to do everything in their power to apprehend him as quickly as possible.

Crime scene investigators discovered a set of tyre tracks near the body. They made plaster-cast impressions of them, the technical equivalent of fingerprinting, and sent them to the lab for analysis and possible future comparison. There the analyst noted that the front and rear right tyres were of standard tread design but the left rear tyre had an unusual design.

The immediate priority for the investigation team was to establish the cause of death and the identity of the victim. The medical examiner established from the autopsy findings that the woman had been strangled, and semen found in the vaginal area established that she had been raped. This confirmed the murder as a sex killing. Like the vampire, the sexual psychopath lusts for blood and begins to crave killing. The sexual thrill he derives is from the control, torture and humiliation of the victim. The one thing he cannot control is his own impulse to kill.

Capt Terry decided to call in the expertise of the FBI to examine the evidence found at the crime scene and from the autopsy. In the lab, the fibre analyst located a red nylon fibre which he concluded probably came from the floor carpeting in the car.

The investigation team now had two important and distinct pieces of the jigsaw, the unusual tyre design and the red fibre originating from the interior of the car which carried the victim to her horrendous end.

The state of the body made it hard to establish the race or age of the woman but the medical examiner suspected that she might have been of Asian descent. The team checked on the computer the missing persons reports for females in the area and one seemed to provide a match for the victim's physical features of height, weight and stature. The team lifted her fingerprints and this, allied with the report, confirmed her identity.

She was Ngeun Thi Long, also known as Lana Long, a twenty-year-old dancer at The Sly Fox lounge in Tampa. Checking her background, the team found that she was a drug addict and may have had to resort to prostitution to feed her habit. She had been seen on a number of occasions getting into cars driven by different men. She was last seen leaving a bar called CC's. Prostitutes leave themselves notoriously vulnerable to predatory killers, particularly if they are hooked on drugs. The murder of one of their profession does not stop them peddling sex to strange men. If the killer was targeting prostitutes, the investigation team knew that it would be even harder to apprehend him. The FBI in particular had a lot of experience in the area and expected the killer to strike again – sooner rather than later.

Just two weeks later a construction worker came across a body near Plant City in Hillsborough County. When the police arrived, investigators discovered similar characteristics with the previous murder. The woman was on her back and a green T-shirt she had been wearing was used to bind her arms. Her wrists had been tied loosely behind her back and a rope had been wrapped three times around her neck which had been cut with a knife. The killer had his calling card, as if he wanted to let investigators know that he had been responsible for the two murders.

Hair and fibre evidence collected on and near the body included several strands of hair and, once again, a red fibre. There were tyre tracks, which were again set in plaster cast impressions, plus a bare footprint in the mud, an impression of which was also made.

The autopsy revealed that the woman had been savagely murdered. There was trauma to the head caused by a large blunt instrument, a large knife cut to the neck, which had severed, and, from the appearance of petechiae, or broken blood vessels, in the eyes, evidence that she had been strangled. She had been dead approximately twelve hours. It was a killing of shocking and unrestrained brutality. The killer was obviously a monster with not a trace of mercy for his victims.

A forensic artist made a composite sketch from postmortem photographs and this, with details of height, weight and colour of hair and eyes was passed to the media. The victim was identified as twenty-two-year-old Michelle Simms, a prostitute and a drug addict.

Back at the FBI lab, special agent Malone examined the crime scene evidence and matched the tyre impressions from the two scenes and the similar red fibres. Investigators were now in no doubt that the same man was responsible for both killings and had used the same car. His modus operandi was that of a serial killer.

The hair found at the scene was not the victim's. It was

racially identified to be Caucasian and came from the head of the killer. Semen samples were of an AB blood type. This was two years before the discovery of DNA fingerprinting and, while the grouping narrowed the search, it could not identify the killer conclusively.

From previous experience, the likelihood of apprehending him quickly was not great. The random killer is often only caught when he slips up or takes too great a risk. Sometimes he is apprehended by pure chance. But the investigation team was building up the evidence which, if he did slip up, would ensure he would be punished for his crimes.

Another forensic tool – a psychological profile of the killer – would help the investigation team to focus on this particular type of suspect, the random killer who, like the father of serial killers Jack the Ripper, displayed his wrath for the female species by targeting prostitutes.

While women working in the sex industry provide convenient prey for the sexual psychopath, that is not the sole reason they are targeted. The savagery of the murders revealed a deep-seated hatred of women and a characterisation of them as whores. The ropes around the neck, the gratuitous violence, showed a deviance that extended beyond the acts of killing and rape. This was the act of a man driven by a compulsion.

He would share other well-established characteristics of such killers, apparently operating normally in society, but be argumentative, self-centred and self-obsessed, traits that would lead him to living the life of a loner. These characteristics would emphasise his inability to fit into the team mode of work and he was most likely to be unemployed, having a history of short-term employment in a variety of jobs. His chosen type of woman would be dependent, easily controlled and would submit to his every whim. This man would be a manipulator and fantasist who, despite the random nature of his killing would have fantasised about the details of what he was going to do to his victims in advance.

The investigation team were armed with the profile by the FBI Behavioural Science Unit in Quantico, Virginia and also advised how to handle the suspect during interrogation if ever apprehended.

Towards the end of June 1984 the severely decomposed body of a young woman was found in an orange grove. The remains were almost liquefied but the medical examiner could determine that death was caused by strangulation. Later identified as twenty-two-year-old Elizabeth Loudenbeck, a factory worker, she in no way fitted the background of the other victims. She had gone for a walk on June 8 from her mobile home and was never seen alive again.

To investigators this random killing did not fit the profile of the serial killer. But there were two small red fibres on her clothing, the significance of which would only emerge later. Had the killer changed his modus operandi and moved away from the red-light district?

In October of the same year another body was found by a ranch hand on a cattle farm near Hillsborough State Park. Facing the ground and lying under barbed wire, the woman's head was covered in maggots. Her clothes were scattered around her. Her panties had been hung on a fence and her bra on a gate, obviously posed. Again the victim had been raped and strangled but there was also a gunshot wound to the back of the head.

Fingerprints were lifted in the morgue and she was identified as a teenage Black girl, Chanel Devon Williams, who was a prostitute. It was the trademark killing with one variation. Trace evidence included red fibres, Caucasian hair but semen of a different grouping. This did not change investigators' views of who was responsible for the murder, however, as the victim, being a prostitute, could have picked up a number of different blood types in semen from different customers.

The tempo of the killing was increasing – a week later another body was found with the victim's clothes scattered around the body. She had been strangled and raped. Identified as prostitute and drug addict Karen Dingsfriend, her clothes contained the tell-tale red fibres. Two weeks later the next victim was found, but had been so long in a ditch that her remains were mummified. She had been strangled but her identity was not established until the killer was caught. She was twenty-two-year-old prostitute Kimberly Kyle Hoops.

In November in the neighbouring Pasco County yet another severely decomposed body, which had been picked at by animals, was found by a woman out horse riding. There was a cord around her neck and the body had been severed, parts scattered around. The hands had been tied. Once more, identification was impossible until the killer was caught. The victim was eighteen-year-old Virginia Johnson, a prostitute who operated in Tampa.

Six days later the next victim was discovered in Tampa. Tampa police called in the Hillsborough investigation team who observed the noose around the neck, the trauma to the head and face. Her legs had been forced open and posed and her clothes scattered around the body. Cause of death was strangulation. Kim Marie Swann was twenty-one years of age and worked as a dancer at The Sly Fox where the first victim also had a job.

The investigation team had accumulated a lot of potentially damning evidence but without a suspect it was useless. Despite the number and frequency of the murders, they did not have even the hint of a suspect. They, and the public, were getting increasingly anxious that more and more young women would be killed.

Profilers told the team that the killer would slip up. A lot of sated serial killers, ironically, feel a sense of relief when finally caught. The investigation team from the Hillsborough County sheriff's office were hoping that the killer was reaching that stage. Some serial killers have bigger appetites than others, but some are insatiable.

No matter how far police forces spread their net, the chances of apprehending the killer would depend on chance and a lucky break because the territory to be covered was simply too vast. The break, however, was to come in a bizzare twist to the murderous saga. On the evening of November 3, seventeen-year-old Lisa McVey was cycling home from work when, in a wooded park area, she was grabbed from her bike and bundled into a car. She was blindfolded and driven away, sure that she was going to be killed.

For a young teenager she displayed a very mature survival instinct telling her abductor she would obey his wishes if he spared her life. He ordered her to take off her clothes and perform oral sex on him. After driving around for a while he brought her back to his apartment where he subjected her to a series of sexual assaults and rape. At one stage he told her that she smelt like a whore and told her that she must have a shower with him. Lisa complied with everything he asked and despite being told to keep her eyes shut during her ordeal managed to take in some of her surroundings. On the way she had tried, when he stopped at a cash point, to take in the location and details of the interior of the car by peeking from under the blindfold.

When later he had sated his considerable sexual appetite, he treated her more gently. Instinctively she knew that she must not anger this predator even in the smallest way or he might turn very nasty.

He brought her back to the car. After driving a distance he let her out of the car and drove away. When she made her way home she told her family what had happened and the police were contacted. The investigators arrived and she gave them a detailed description of her attacker, a white male in his early to mid-thirties, slightly overweight with dark brown hair and a small moustache.

She gave a description of the car but could remember nothing about the carpet or its colour. Considering that she had suffered a terrible ordeal lasting just over twenty-four hours the young woman was remarkably composed, a demeanour that had probably saved her life. Her clothes were taken for examination and sent with other rape evidence to the FBI laboratory. Once again, the red fibres were found and the investigation team knew that Lisa had been abducted by the serial killer.

Why did he release this victim? Was he running out of murder steam? Did he purposely leave a marker that might lead police to his door? He had not even warned his victim not to contact police. He knew full well that she would and this could lead to his capture.

But in the interim his compulsion led him to kill another young woman. However, the hunt for him was on in earnest and the investigators had for the first time got some very solid leads to follow.

Two weeks after Lisa McVey's abduction, a car that fitted the description she gave, a red Dodge Magnum, was spotted by a detective patrol car in traffic. The car was pulled in and the detectives checked the car licence. The man matched Lisa's description. His name was Robert Joe Long and his address was within the area where the team were looking for the serial killer's living accommodation.

The detectives knew they could not arrest him without due cause but when they told him that they were looking for a robbery suspect, he agreed to be photographed. He was then let go and immediately the investigation team set about putting together the parts of the evidential jigsaw they had assembled.

An ATM withdrawal he had made was found to be in the same time frame that Lisa McVey had described. Surveillance teams were scrambled to log every movement of Robert Long, better known as Bobby, not only as part of the investigation but also to make sure another young woman was not killed while sufficient evidence was presented to make an arrest. Once presented, a court order was obtained for Long's arrest on charges of kidnap and sexual battery in relation to Lisa's abduction, and another order for the impoundment and search of his car.

As soon as Long was in custody, crime scene investigators scoured every inch of the car and sent samples to the FBI lab for examination and comparison. A sample of the floor carpet was found to match the red fibres already collected from a number of the crime scenes. The team knew that they had the serial killer but they had to make sure that the body of evidence would convict Bobby Joe Long. Despite the obvious links between the suspect and the crime scenes and the victims, his responsibility and guilt had to be proved to the court beyond all reasonable doubt. Nothing in the matter of murder is easy or straightforward, including its aftermath.

The forensic team moved into Long's apartment where they found a hair accessory that Lisa had left behind. They found pornography as well as photos of Long raping victims –

Long playing a leading role in his own perverted creation. There were also items of women's clothing, some probably belonging to victims which Long kept for his sexual gratification as well as being trophies of his crimes.

During his interrogation it emerged that Long was an unemployed X-ray technician who had been married and was the father of two children but was divorced for a number of years. He admitted to the abduction and rape of Lisa McVey. He also confirmed the FBI profilers' prediction about a deliberate slip-up: he said he knew that when he let Lisa McVey go free it was just a matter of time until the police arrived on his doorstep.

The interrogating detectives who had been briefed knew that they should maintain a firm and authoritative line of questioning without being aggressive. Pyschopaths respond to such aggression by closing up. The detectives then brought up the subject of the other victims and told Long of the physical evidence that linked him to the crime scenes and the victims, specifically the tyre mark impressions and the carpet fibres. Long at first denied any knowledge of the crimes but when faced with the incontrovertible forensic connections indicated that he might need a lawyer. At that point the interrogators should have stopped the interview to allow the suspect his constitutional right to have a lawyer present. They did not and this would come back to haunt the prosecution during the trial process.

Long then confessed to his involvement in the series of brutal murders which the investigators knew about plus some others that they were not aware of. By releasing Lisa McVey, he knew it was the beginning of the end for him but he said that he did not care about being apprehended at that stage. Earlier he had thought of going to a doctor but thought that this would lead to his being arrested and he wasn't ready for that eventuality just then. He claimed that he felt sick inside.

He described his killings in simple terms with no hint of remorse. In the case of Elizabeth Loudenbeck he had thought about letting her go until 'she jerked me around'. He strangled her with a rope, took her purse and bank card, used it and threw it away. Long described the last moments of his victims as if he was reading a shopping list.

The detectives wanted the facts and Long gave them coldly and dispassionately. While strangling Karen Dingsfriend in an orange grove he heard dogs barking. He stuck the girl in the boot of the car, drove to another location and finished the job. When asked if he knew anything about the disappearance of Vicky Elliott, a twenty-one-year-old who had gone missing the previous month while walking to her midnight shift, he admitted the killing. She had accepted a lift from him, but when he began to assault her, she produced a pair of scissors. This sent him into a rage and he strangled her. He indicated on a map the spot where he had dumped her body. When the investigating team found the skeletal remains of the victim, the tell-tale red fibres were at the scene. Beside the bones which surrounded the spot where the vagina should be, rested a pair of scissors. Long had mutilated his victim's sexual organ.

There began a lengthy series of trials in Florida. Long's guilt was not in question but legal issues such as the detectives going beyond their legal remit and transgressing the suspect's legal rights during the initial interrogation greatly stretched the trial process through appeals and retrials.

There was also the question of whether Long, being a psychotic, was responsible for his actions. An army of health experts were introduced to confirm or deny this theory, which boils down to the simple matter of whether the defendant could distinguish between right and wrong and if he knew that he was doing wrong when committing the crimes.

The prosecution claimed that he did and in the end the juries believed that to be the case. He received two death sentences, thirty-four life sentences and an additional 693 years on associated charges. Long was incarcerated on death row.

One of the most important pieces of evidence that put this serial killer where he belonged was a red fibre.

6

POSTMORTEM

The postmortem, known as the autopsy in the US, is performed mainly to establish in the forensic field the cause of suspicious death. The pathologist or medical examiner does not interpret the evidence but must find that evidence, preserve it and scientifically establish how and what caused the death.

The pathologist's modus operandi includes a visual inspection, an injury inspection, an internal examination, the reconciliation of all exhibits, and the presentation of findings to the investigation team and other experts. The postmortem report and the evidence of the examiner is a vital and important component of the investigative and legal processes.

There is a visual examination of both the clothed body and the naked corpse. In both cases the body is photographed with special attention to the injured areas. When the clothes are removed, each item is air dried and packaged separately for forensic examination and stored if needed to be used as exhibits in court.

Swabs are taken to test for the presence of gunpowder residue. The configuration of bullet wounds provides telling evidence. When the discharge of the gun is from a distance, a bullet hole occurs with no other residue. If the weapon is held directly to the skin, the bullet hole is accompanied by a burn caused by the heat and flare of the shot. Most guns used in a close-range shooting leave a stippling effect on the skin, like small tattoo marks. Also, a close-contact shooting to a bony area of the body such as the skull leaves a star pattern, usually found in execution-style killings with the shot delivered to the back of the head.

Knife wounds also leave distinctive identifying markings depending on the size and shape of the weapon and whether the edge is smooth or serrated. A single-edged blade makes a different-shaped wound to a double-edged weapon.

Visible marks on the skin and eye appearance are particularly important in the case of death by strangulation. The use of rope leaves very distinctive markings on the skin. The shape of the marks can indicate the method used: a garrotte leaves a horizontal line, while a hanging in a suicide case leaves a mark with an upward slant. Petechiae, or broken blood vessels in the eyes, provide confirmation that the victim has been strangled.

Part of the visual examination is to search for trace evidence such as hairs, fibres or foreign DNA. The use of special lighting and lasers can detect hairs, pollen, saliva, blood, semen and fingerprints on flesh. Head hair is combed for traces of such evidence and body openings are examined for foreign objects, trace evidence and DNA. The hands are fingerprinted and nail scrapings taken to determine if there is trace evidence such as skin, hair or blood. Where sexual contact or rape is suspected, a special rape kit is used for evidence collection.

Notes are taken of the injuries and the general physical appearance of the body along with the hair and eye colour.

When the visual examination of the body is complete and all relevant evidence photographed and documented, the body is carefully washed in preparation for the internal examination. The body is then laid on its back with a stabilising block placed under the head.

The pathologist starts with a Y incision, which is a cut from each shoulder meeting at the base of the breast bone, the letter shape completed at the lower extremity by a cut from the base of the breast bone to the pubic bone. This incision exposes the internal organs and allows the examiner easy access.

The pathologist then uses an instrument to cut the ribs and the collarbone to expose the chest for examination. Blood is drawn from the heart and it, along with other organs such as the lungs, is examined, measured, weighed and sectioned. Samples are kept for further laboratory testing.

The stomach and intestines are opened and the contents examined, the digestive condition of which can help determine the time of death. The liver, spleen and pancreas are weighed and subjected to individual examination. The pelvic region is then looked at and fluid from the bladder removed for analysis. The presence, for example, of drugs or alcohol can be determined.

In women the reproductive organs are examined for signs

of pregnancy, previous and current, and also of sexual interference. If there is semen present, a sample is recovered for analysis.

When this stage of the examination is complete organs are returned to the cavities in the body. The next and last stage is the examination of the head. A single incision is made in the scalp behind the head from ear to ear and the skin is carefully folded back to expose the skull and possible breaks or blunt force trauma. Then, using a high-powered oscillating drill, the pathologist opens the skull and uses a chisel to pry off the skull cap. He or she lifts out the brain, examines it, weighs it and sections it for microscopic examination. When completed, the brain is returned to the skull cavity, the skull replaced and the skin replaced. The pathologist then sews up the incisions. The postmortem is finished and all tissues and samples are forwarded to the laboratory for analysis.

If the pathologist or medical examiner were presented with bodies in the same general state then their work would be fairly straightforward but just like murder, nothing is that simple or the same. The victim could be recently deceased, slightly decomposed or totally decomposed with nothing but bones remaining, not one ounce of flesh visible. There could be a situation in which the examiner is faced with an exhumation months or decades after burial. Depending on the ground in which the body was buried, its state could vary from being well preserved to total decomposition and skeletal remains.

Embalming presents particular challenges for the

pathologist. During the embalming process blood is drained from the body and replaced with a formaldehyde compound that sometimes contains pink dyes to improve the appearance of the body. This process preserves the body for a time but radically changes the chemistry.

The pathologist is a medical witness of fact. More often than not investigators and courts will rely on the postmortem findings to come to a proper conclusion in a case.

One of the most famous practitioners of pathology is Dr Michael Baden former New York medical examiner who during his forty-year career conducted more than 20,000 postmortem examinations. From 1960 until 1985 he was New York's medical examiner and subsequently co-director for the medicolegal investigative unit of NY State Police.

In the savage Nicole Brown Simpson and Ronald Goldman murders, OJ Simpson's lawyer Robert Shapiro phoned Baden and asked him to come to Simpson's home. In the company of criminalist Henry Lee he arrived five days after the murder. After a call from the police the suspect left the house and was involved in the famous car chase down the freeway.

Baden subsequently examined the crime scene investigation and learned how many mistakes had been made, not just by the investigators but also by the forensic medical team in the mishandling of the bodies. They were not extraordinary mistakes but very elementary misjudgements that should have never taken place.

One inexplicable mistake was that a medical examiner was not notified at the time the bodies were discovered. For some reason the investigating officers waited for ten hours thus ruling out the vital preliminary postmortem examination when accurate conclusions about the time of death could have been deduced from the postmortem state of the bodies.

The problem in Dr Baden's opinion was the way death investigation was practised in the US.

> When you look back on the history of murder investigations in this country, in most places we use the same system we used in colonial days. The people who do investigations are elected and they often have no medical expertise. We get upset about the handling of cases such as Nicole Brown Simpson and JonBenet Ramsey because we think these cases weren't investigated according to community standards. Sadly, they were in fact handled according to community standards, which are pretty poor. We have around fifty murders a day in the US and most are investigated at the crime scene by people not competent to do it. Autopsies, too, are often done by physicians not trained to do them.

While Baden's high standards are not met in every case there has been a huge improvement worldwide in investigative methods – on the ground, in the offices of the medical examiner and in the laboratories – perhaps because of such high-profile cases as OJ Simpson. Authorities are determined not to make the same mistakes.

Pathologists have an important contribution to make in the successful solving of crimes, especially murder. Their particular way of investigation and vision can turn the obvious into something completely different, the very opposite to 'Elementary, my dear Watson.' In short, the pathologist could be described as a death detective.

7

BONES AND BUGS

There are other branches in the detection of death, most notably the forensic anthropologists and entomologists, whose science as with the pathologists can prove that victims are not silenced in death and can point the finger to the guilty from the grave.

While anthropology is defined as the study of human origins, in the forensic field there are a wide number of disciplines involved. The FBI Law Enforcement Bulletin of July 1990 stated that the science of forensic anthropology includes archaeological excavation; examination of hair, insects, plant materials and footprints; determination of elapsed time since death; facial reproduction; photographic superimposition; detection of anatomical variants; and analysis of past injury and medical treatment.

In practice the forensic anthropologist primarily helps to identify a victim from the available evidence which could be reduced to a number of bones. The field has developed over the past since a legendary figure Dr Bill Bass, founder of the University of Tennessee Centre for Forensic Anthropology, had to conduct experiments in his own kitchen. Investigators had brought him the remains of a corpse found by the roadside and wanted a description to help identify the victim and to disseminate details through the media to help their investigation.

To refine my estimate of age and to gauge the woman's stature, I needed to remove the remaining tissue from the bones. Short of leaving the skull and femur outdoors and allowing insects and scavengers to pick the bones clean – a slow process – the only good way to clean the bones was to simmer them in a covered steam vat for the better part of the day, then scrub off the softened tissue with a toothbrush (not my own personal one).

Needless to say my wife wasn't thrilled when she arrived home to the stench of cooking flesh and found a decaying human skull and femur simmering in her eight-quart kettle.

That was just a day in the life of Dr Bass far back in 1962, when there were very few of his kind in the detection game and the facilities and tools for the job were just as scarce. His lab was equipped to study skeletons and bone fragments and not what might be termed more healthy corpses with meat on the bones.

He was later convinced that more crimes could be solved if researchers in the field better understood how bodies decompose. In 1997 Bass established the Body Farm where researchers could study decomposing bodies under a variety of conditions. It seemed like a bizarre idea more out of fiction than fact, a subject not for the faint hearted.

On the site at the edge of the university centre, at any time there are as many as fifty corpses in various states of decomposition scattered throughout the two-acre wooded piece of land. Some are stuffed in the trunks of cars, others lie in the open under the sun and many are buried in the shade of trees.

Most of the bodies have been donated for research while others are the unclaimed bodies of people who had either no relatives or had lost touch with them.

On the Body Farm researchers test the soil to find residue from the corpses. As bodies decompose, they leak fatty acids, the breakdown products of muscle and fat. The profiles of these acids change as time passes, and so analysis of them can pinpoint how long a body has been lying in a particular place.

Bones are the territory of the anthropologist and can reveal a lot about a body: what injuries were inflicted, how the death occurred and the age of the victim. There are equally bizarre practices in the lab as there are on the Body Farm. Sometimes when bones need to be cleaned, a species of beetle is employed to do the job. These carrion beetles will only eat leathery soft tissues and will not touch the bone.

Simple boiling and cleansing with a detergent is also a method used. Bones are cooked just like meat in a pot to strip the flesh from the bone.

Examination of teeth can reveal age if the remains belong to a child or adolescent. Areas of the femur can indicate age in cases where teeth are missing. The skull and the pelvic bones can determine sex. Female skulls show some differences to male skulls but the pelvic girdle – a woman's is wider than a man's – provides a positive identification of sex.

Height can be gauged from the long bones of the legs but when they are not present, a range of heights can be established from as little as a single finger or foot bone.

Sketch artists draw pictures of criminals based on witness descriptions and anthropologists do the same thing utilising skeletal remains. Forensic artists build models of what a dead person might have looked like, making a plaster cast of the skull and covering it with clay to imitate flesh.

Computer graphics are also being used to create images. Researchers scan a skull to create a 3D computer model. Certain sites on the skull reveal qualities of flesh that would have covered it. Software adds flesh of appropriate thickness adjusting for variables, such as sex, age and ethnic background. An animated head can be produced with life-like levels of detail.

The face can be aged or created youthful, based on well-established growth patterns. Ears, for example, get longer with age so, given the photograph of a child, the anthropologist can adjust each feature to age the subject and create an image of what the subject would look like years later.

Computer graphics can offer a series of images that can be adjusted in an instant, and a number of possibilities printed out for investigators. Digitalised superimpositions of photographs of individuals onto the skull is also an exciting and accurate route to identification.

The number of disciplines involved in forensic anthropology is large and top expert Dr Arpad Vass of the University of Tennessee says, 'The more multi-disciplinary you are, the better the crime investigator you are.' He illustrates this with a case that could be straight out of TV.

A man kills his wife. His girlfriend watches as he places the body in a fifty-five gallon drum, douses it with kerosene and lights a match. He dumps the burnt remains onto the edge of an empty field. Three years later the couple split up. The woman went to the police and described the murder. Investigators needed forensic corroboration and went to the scene of the crime but found no trace of anything. They tested the soil but found nothing.

One of the investigators had an idea. He sawed off the limb from a tree at the edge of the field, traced the tree's annual growth which showed rings back three years before at the time of the crime. In the lab he was able to isolate kerosene within that ring. The suspect was eventually convicted even though no body was ever found.

Entomological experts study the behaviour of bug and insect life which can provide vital evidence for investigators. When a body begins to decompose in an open space, it sets off insect activity. Female blowflies have such a keen sense of smell that as much as a mile away they can locate the site of death to feed off the corpse.

As far back as 1235 AD a Chinese investigator wrote a book

about detection of the times. Sung Tz'u predicated in his findings the beginnings of forensic science, without of course the benefits of science, proving that the art of detection fundamentally has not changed throughout the centuries: the eye of the detective must be constantly focused. A murder had taken place in a small village and the victim had been slashed to death. After the usual investigative method of questioning, nothing had emerged.

The local detective, for want of a better word, asked all the villagers to bring in their sickles for examination. They were laid down on the ground and soon a swarm of flies landed on one of the sickles. This, the detective deduced, was because remnants of the victim's tissue were on the weapon.

Faced with the evidence, the killer broke down and confessed to the crime. It was a thirteenth century example of a murder scenario that could occur today: an uncooperative suspect confesses when presented with incontrovertible forensic evidence.

It was widely believed that rotting flesh produced its own flies and maggots, as if the infestation was internally combusted, until experiments in the seventeenth century proved otherwise – the body inexorably invites the infestation by the process of death itself and decomposition.

Bugs, flies and insects can provide an accurate picture of where and when a person is killed.

In 1855 the body of a baby was discovered in a house in France. It had been hidden behind a plaster mantle. The pathologist established during the postmortem that the infestation of the insects pointed to an earlier time than that of the occupants who had been accused of the crime. The previous occupants were found to be the guilty parties.

As well as blowflies, a variety of other insects are drawn to a dead body and colonise it in a very logical fashion, known as succession. This development provides the forensic entomologist with a graphic picture of the circumstances surrounding the death. Each species of insect progresses through its life cycle at very predictable stages which can be tracked under laboratory conditions by the entomologist.

The bug's life in a body is very easy to follow from the laying of eggs through the different stages of maturity, taking into account climatic conditions and the stages of decomposition of the body. The outside temperature is important to the maggot's progress, heat speeds it up while cold slows it down, so the expert keeps a keen eye on the reports from weather stations in the vicinity of the area where the body was discovered. Like all aspects of detection, it is a calculated balancing act.

Not all the bugs are attracted to the body at the same time, some prefer the freshly decayed, others the well decayed. Some don't feed on the actual body but on the moulds formed on them or on other insects that are already on the body. They literally come in waves. Their activity, like the decaying process of the body, follows a well-documented path and the body detective can track and monitor them all in their varied species and life progression.

8
BLOOD

Blood is the most common and perhaps most important evidence in the world of criminal justice today. There is no substitute for it, whether for medical or forensic purposes. Its presence always links suspect, victim and the scene of violence.

Blood-stain patterns tell a lot about the position and movement during the crime, who struck whom first, in what manner, and how many times. This destroys most alibi and self-defence arguments for crime or, at the very least, it trips up most suspects in their explanation of what happened. Over the years, criminals have tried many ingenious ways to hide, clean up, and remove blood evidence, but it's an area where criminal justice technology has always stayed one step ahead of them.

Determination of the type and characteristics of blood, blood testing, blood-stain examination, as well as preparation of testimony or presentations at a trial are the main functions of a forensic serologist. They may also analyse semen, saliva and other body fluids and be involved in DNA typing.

Serologists can provide evidence with some probability linking a single individual, and that individual only, to a blood stain.

Blood-stain pattern analysis is a powerful forensic tool for detection and investigation. If the investigator understands how blood behaves when it exits the body, and how it reacts when it contacts a surface, then an attempt can be made to understand what happened and to determine if and how a crime occurred.

The smaller the drops of blood, the faster they were moving. A fog of tiny droplets suggests high velocity – a gunshot or explosive device. Large drops are associated with low-impact injuries like a punch. Mid-speed droplets almost always relate to the impact of a knife or blunt object. Slightly bigger droplets result from severe beatings by hand.

Looking at the drops, the investigator can deduce the direction in which the drop of blood was travelling. The angle from which it was travelling is then worked out. A spray of blood results from most gunshot wounds. The spray on entry is called 'forward spatter', the spray from the exit wound is called 'backward spatter'. If there is someone or something between the wound and the surface that would normally catch blood spatter, the blood lands on the person or object, not on the surface behind them. That break in the pattern, called 'shadowing' or 'ghosting', fixes the position of a person or object now missing from the scene.

Wet blood has more value than dried blood because more tests can be run on it. For example, alcohol and drug content can be determined from wet blood only. Blood begins to dry after three to five minutes' exposure to air. Blood at the crime scene can be in the form of pools, drops, smears or crusts. Drops of blood tell the height and angle from which the blood fell. The forensic science of blood spatter analysis concludes that blood which falls perpendicularly to the floor from a distance of up to two feet makes a circular drop with frayed edges (sunburst pattern).

A blood smear on the wall or floor tells the direction of force of the blow. The direction of force is always in the direction towards the tail, or smaller, end of the smear or spatter. In other words, the largest area of the smear is the point of origin. Blood crusts need to be tested to make sure that they are in fact blood.

The detailed terminology which follows, describing blood-stain patterns, gives an indication of their importance as an investigative tool in forensic science.

Angle of impact: The angle at which a blood droplet strikes a surface.

Arterial gushing: The large pattern of blood that is created when blood escapes an artery under pressure. The increase and decrease in blood pressure is apparent.

Arterial spurts: Large patterns created under pressure, but with less volume. There is usually more distinctive evidence of blood pressure rising and falling.

Clot: A mass of blood and other contaminants caused through clotting mechanisms.

Cast-off stains: Blood that has been thrown from a secondary object (weapon or hand) onto a target other than the impact site.

Drop patterns: Characteristic patterns present when blood drips into standing, wet blood.

Expiratory blood: Blood which is spattered onto a target, as a result of breathing. This typically occurs when an injury is sustained to the throat, mouth or an airway.

Impact site: Usually the point on the body that received the blow or applied force.

Origin: The point from where the blood spatter came.

Parent drop: The droplet from which smaller spatters originated.

Projected blood: Blood under pressure which strikes a target.

Satellite spatters: Small drops of blood that break off from the parent spatter when the parent droplet strikes a target surface.

Shadowing/ghosting/void: A pattern that helps to place an object or body at the scene. An area lacks blood even though areas surrounding it show blood.

Skeletonised stain: The pattern left when an object moves through a partially dried stain, removing some blood but leaving an outline of the stain intact.

Spatter: Blood stains created from the application of force or energy to the area where the blood is.

Spines: The pointed edges of a stain that radiate out to form the spatter.

Splash: Pattern created when a volume of blood in excess of 1 ml strikes a surface at a low to medium velocity.

Swipe: The transfer of blood onto a target surface by a

bloody object that is usually moving sideways.

Transfer pattern: The pattern created when a wet, bloody object comes in contact with a surface, leaving a pattern that has the features of the object, making it useful for identifying the object.

Target: The surface on which the blood lands.

Wipe: Pattern created when a secondary target moves through an existing wet blood stain on some other object.

The leading expert on blood-stain analysis is American Herbert Leon MacDonnell. He was the first to introduce blood-stain evidence into the courts of twenty-three states and also into European countries.

He was involved in a case as far back as the 1970s in Oregon which involved an elderly widow Ellen Anderson who had been severely assaulted. The suspect was a young woman called Lesley Harley who had acted as the old woman's help. The prosecution claimed she had a problem with her employer's will and had attacked her with a poker.

The blood trail demonstrated that Ellen had been beaten in a number of rooms in the house but had miraculously survived to tell the tale. The defence claimed that Harley had helped the victim upstairs into bed and began to telephone a doctor for help. The blood spatter on the ceiling they claimed was as a result of the old woman shaking her head in an effort to say no to the help offered.

MacDonnell established that the spatter pattern could not have happened in the manner described, it must have come from a beating downwards on the head. In a laboratory experiment with a model acting as the victim shaking her head saturated with blood he proved that none of the spatter ended up on the ceiling. The jury believed his expert testimony and the accused went to jail.

There are times when such expertise is called for by defence and prosecution counsels but for one reason or another is not utilised, often to the detriment of the case. Such vital evidence can lead not only to the successful conviction of killers but can also prove the innocence of someone wrongly convicted.

That such compelling forensic evidence could ever be excluded in a case is extraordinary. Witnesses may make mistakes or lie, forensic evidence never does.

MacDonnell's expertise helped to release a woman who had served nine years for the murder of her husband. In October 1987 William Mowbray, a car dealer in Brownsville, Texas, was found dead in his home with a single gunshot wound to his right temple. His wife was the prime suspect. The following month MacDonnell was contacted by the local prosecutor to assess vital evidence, a long-sleeved, white nightgown that Mowbray's wife Susie was wearing on the night of the apparent killing. MacDonnell found under microscopic examination no trace of blood on the garment. On further examination of the scene he discovered very fine blood stains on the headboard of the bed where the victim was found. They were to the side of where the body had been. The sheet contained backward spattered blood.

Blood

Because MacDonnell found no blood on Susie Mowbray's nightgown, it indicated that she could not have been directly involved in her husband's death. But the prosecution team ignored that evidence and found another expert who, using luminol, apparently found blood spatters on the nightgown. MacDonnell's evidence inexplicably was not used in court and Susie Mowbray was convicted of her husband's murder. Wrongly.

Over six years later an appeal lawyer contacted MacDonnell and at a hearing the judge decided, as a result of his evidence being suppressed, to order a new trial. At that trial in 1998 MacDonnell took the stand and his evidence, along with that of another witness who said that William Mowbray had threatened to kill himself shortly before his death, led to the acquittal of Susie Mowbray.

MacDonnell like many other experts was dragged into the high-profile OJ Simpson case. He was sent over 100 photographs from the crime scene. Three things struck him: the enormous amount of blood at the scene, the small space in which the murders took place and the blood droplets on Nicole Brown Simpson's back. He wondered in this last instance why that blood evidence had not been collected and sent to the lab for analysis.

MacDonnell carried out his own reconstruction using a model stand-in for Nicole to explain the origin and pattern of blood on the victim's back, the angles and the impact. But his evidence was ultimately not used; it was left behind in the rush of the more important issues of the so-called trial. He and crime scene investigators all over the world knew that this case had in fact been lost at the crime scene.

Blood evidence is central to an investigation, and can be responsible for successful convictions, as long as the right experts are involved from beginning to end.

9

THE BLACK DAHLIA MURDER

The morning of January 15, 1947, was cool and overcast in Los Angeles. It was one of those grey, nondescript days that most citizens would want to forget. It had been like that for a couple of weeks and the *LA Times* had been debating how much airborne pollution, car exhaust fumes and factory waste had contributed to the leaden skies. The people got on about their business; there was always something to be done and addressed, whatever the weather or the dangers of pollution.

The stink of corruption hung as heavily as the smog over the City of Angels. This was a place where anything and anyone could be fixed and bought as long as the price was right. Gangsters were big and powerful in the thirties and forties and ran their own divided territories, their tentacles touching lawyers and so-called legitimate businessmen, politicians and even the police and sheriff's departments.

It may have been a grey day but it was not going to be one that Los Angeles would forget for a long time. Especially not a young married woman, by the name of Betty Bersinger, who was busy that morning with household chores and minding her young daughter after her husband had gone to work.

When her chores were done, Betty decided that she would go to a local shop where she could get repairs done to her daughter's shoes. Just after ten o'clock Betty, accompanied by her three-year-old daughter Anne, left their home in Norton and walked south along Norton Avenue. As they passed a vacant lot the little girl pointed to a clump of bushes and her mother saw a glimpse of white. At first she thought it was an abandoned mannequin but a closer look shocked her. It was a body that in every way resembled a mannequin which had been broken and abandoned.

Not knowing whether the person was alive or dead, she ran to a nearby home and called the university division police station, saying that there was a drunk lying in the weeds. Dispatch assigned the call to a patrol unit: 'possible 390 [drunk] down at the lot at 39th and Norton Avenue.' From the tenor of the call it seemed just routine: a street drunk passed out in the undergrowth on a vacant lot. But it was a quiet morning and the call-out would put in some shift time for the patrolmen.

When the call went out, it wasn't just the patrol that responded but also a number of newspaper reporters cruising around the city in search of a story. Most self-respecting reporters had powerful radios and top-class antennas plugged into the police radio frequencies, and everyone wanted to be at the scene of the crime first. *Los Angeles Examiner* reporter Gene Fowler and photographer Felix Paegel tuned into the dispatch call just as it was broadcast over police radio and were first to arrive at the scene.

Fowler got out of the car and, as he approached the clump of bushes, saw the ivory white outline of a body. There is something, he remarked to himself, about a dead body that you could not mistake. He moved carefully forward, as he said later, as if the corpse might jump up and run at him.

While his partner Paegel was unloading his photographic equipment from the boot of the car, Fowler's adrenalin was pumping. Here was a body; he was on the spot, going to have the story first, a situation that sends the ink blood coursing through the veins of any reporter, anywhere, any time. But, then, he had no idea that he was on the scene of one of the most infamous, intriguing and mysterious murder cases in the canons of American crime.

He was staring at the body of a young woman, shocking enough, but the sight confronting him forced a double take. The corpse was in two separate pieces, a clump of wild grass in between. Fowler began to hyperventilate. In between taking fast, short breaths, he managed to shout to the photographer, 'Jesus, Felix, this woman is cut in half.' He could hardly believe his eyes. Both halves were facing upwards and her arms were extended above her head. Her legs were splayed apart. There was evidence of apparent torture: both breasts were marked by knife wounds, and a deep slash ran between the victim's navel and the pubic hair. Between the severed torso and the lower half, grass sprouted. Even in a city used to crime and violence, this was a gross, unprecedented and unnatural sight.

There were slashes at each side of the victim's mouth,

extending to her ears giving a grotesque clown-like twist to her pretty face. There was a shadow of a death smile but it radiated pain. As he knelt over the body he noticed that her fingernails were short and bitten and her hair had been dyed jet black. Her translucent blue eyes were half open and Fowler closed them.

The reporter's action in closing her eyes would now be interpreted as unforgivable tampering with evidence, but could be explained by his human naivety. Fowler was in a shocked daze but was awoken by the flashes from his colleague's camera. After a couple of shots of him taken beside the body, he moved away from the bizarre scene, possessed of a sense of unreality, and yet the evidence was there in its fulsome awfulness, a frozen immovable image of death in its most brutal and twisted form. An image created by human depravity in its most extreme expression.

But the parameters of the job dictated that the professionals had to get on with the job and, for the moment, suspend the disbelief. Paegel took a series of photographs which appeared later that day in the *Los Angeles Examiner* but, through re-touching, spared the readers the real horror of what had been recorded. The photo artist covered up the lower half of the victim's body with an airbrushed blanket. The gruesome facial wounds were covered up by removing the deep slashes on either side of the mouth.

More detailed police crime-scene photographs verify that the body was clearly bisected at the waist. The two separate halves lie in close proximity, the upper torso placed asymmetrically twelve inches from the lower portion and offset to the left by about six inches. Both of the victim's arms are raised above the head, the right arm at a forty-five degree angle away from the body, then bent at the elbow to form a ninety degree angle. The left arm extends at a similar angle away from the body and then bends again to form a second ninety degree angle.

This was no ordinary dumping of a body. The precise positioning emphasised the humiliation suffered by the unknown victim who was then robbed of all dignity in death. Both reporter and photographer wondered what this young woman could have done to invite such utter physical devastation. And who could be responsible for the calculated butchery and dumping of the body of a young, and obviously once beautiful, woman.

The police patrol arrived and after presenting his ID Fowler walked away from the scene, found a phone booth and sent in his story to city editor James Richardson.

LAPD captain Jack Donohue, after receiving a call from the first patrolmen to arrive, sent down two of his best detectives Harry Hansen and Finis Brown to the crime scene to take charge of the investigation.

Hansen had twenty-one years' service including eleven in homicide. He had already seen one corpse that morning, an elderly man who died of natural causes in a rooming house. There had been no signs of a struggle or anything out of order which might point to a suspicious death. For the detectives it was a simple matter of signing off the lonely demise of an old man. Hansen and his partner Brown were questioning the landlord and waiting for the coroner to arrive when the call came.

'Sounds bad,' Donohue warned. The two detectives could not have imagined just how bad.

By the time they arrived at 11.05 a.m., not only did they have to contend with groups of reporters and photographers, but also with uniformed officers from adjacent divisions. They called in lab men, a technical team including forensic photographers, and an ambulance to remove the body when the on-scene investigation was completed.

Word had spread like wildfire and the scene was swarming with interested parties. No previous Los Angeles murder scene had attracted such a huge reaction and presence. From a forensic point of view it was a disaster as the scene was being trampled on, so contaminating and compromising any evidence that may have been in the immediate vicinity of the body.

Hansen and Brown were not happy with the huge media presence but there was an unholy alliance at the time between the press who wanted to sell newspapers and the top echelons of the LAPD who needed to enhance their careers. Crime was a big part of that commercial process. The detectives knew the score. If they wanted information held back after a crime or murder, the newspapers would honour the request as long as there was a news story payback down the line. And when it suited the investigators, they could leak information which could prove invaluable in flushing out a suspect or in getting more cooperation from the public. This arrangement would create an important dimension to this investigation.

The forensic team attempted to collect whatever physical evidence they could find. It included a paper cement bag with small traces of what appeared to be diluted blood on it. This bag was lying just six inches above the victim's outstretched right hand. One detective speculated that it had been used to carry the two sections of the body from a car which had parked by the pavement next to the grassy lot. Police noticed a vehicle's tyre prints at the kerb's edge close to the body. There was also a bloody heel-print from what was believed to be a man's shoe. These important pieces of evidence, it was established later, were not secured or photographed by the on-scene investigative team.

Detectives Hansen and Brown determined that, due to the lack of blood at the scene, the killer had committed the crime elsewhere, then transported both halves of the body by car to the empty lot at Norton. Since there was no identifying evidence from personal belongings, the victim was listed as Jane Doe Number 1.

The body was eventually removed from the scene for postmortem examination. The following morning, Dr Federic Newbarr, the chief medical examiner for the County of Los Angeles performed the autopsy. His preliminary findings showed the cause of death to be 'haemorrhage and shock due to concussion of the brain and lacerations of the face, and the trauma to the head and face were the result of multiple blows using a blunt instrument.'

The medical examiner concluded that a sharp, thin-bladed instrument, consistent with a surgeon's scalpel, had been used to perform the division of the body. Dr Newbarr, in his notes, observed that the incision was made through the abdomen and then through a disk between the second and third lumbar vertebrae. The bisection had been carried out with such precision that it must have been the work of someone trained in surgical procedures.

More horrific details discovered during the postmortem gave further clues to the monstrous and perverted nature of the killer but were withheld from the press and the public at that time, for good reason, by the investigative team.

The medical examiner's estimate set the time of death as being within a twenty-four hour period prior to the discovery of the body, thus establishing the time of the murder sometime after 10 a.m on January 14, 1947.

Who was the victim and why was she murdered in such a horrendous and vicious fashion? And by whom? The first question would soon be answered but the second and third are the subject of speculation to this day in what came to be famously known as the Black Dahlia murder.

The hunt was on to find the identity of the victim. When some details of the autopsy findings were leaked to the press, not only Los Angeles but the entire country was obsessed with the murder, which became a nationwide phenomenon driven by front-page headlines and radio reports.

The press were as keen as the police investigators to discover who the victim was. A cosy relationship had developed between press and police and it was in the interests of both parties that they help each other.

On the day after the murder the *Los Angeles Examiner* published a questionnaire:

DO YOU KNOW A MISSING GIRL WHO CHEWED HER FINGERNAILS? IF SO SHE MAY BE THE VICTIM OF YESTERDAY'S MUTILATION OR SLAYING.

The dead girl's description:
Age: Between 15 and 16 years
Weight: 118 pounds
Eyes: Grey blue or grey green
Nose: Small, turned-up
Ears: Small lobes
Eyelashes: Virtually colourless
Hair: Hennaed, but originally dark brown growing out
Foot size: $6^{1}/_{2}$
Toenails: Enamelled pink
Scars: $3^{1}/_{2}$ inch operational scar on right side of the back; $1^{1}/_{2}$ inch scar on right side of abdomen (possible appendectomy); vaccination scar on left thigh; small scar on left knee and another above the knee.
Moles: Six small moles on back of neck below collar line; another on small of back.
General description: Rather well developed, small bones with trim legs.

At this stage *the Los Angeles Examiner* was well ahead of the media posse and James Richardson, the city editor, had what turned out to be an inspirational idea. He knew that the fingerprints of the victim had been lifted by the technical team and in a meeting with LAPD detectives he made an offer to fax the prints through the paper's communication network to the Washington bureau. There, FBI agents would be present to transfer the fingerprints to the records section for identification. The quid pro quo was that the *Examiner* would be first to carry the identity of the victim. The idea was immediately accepted as the police were just as hungry for the information.

At 11 a.m. on January 16 the pictures were received by the FBI's identification division. Within fifty-six minutes the identification was established and matched to two fingerprint cards previously on a file bearing the name of Elizabeth Short. Despite the fact that two of the impressions were missing entirely and three others were badly blurred, FBI fingerprint experts were able to make identification by searching all fingerprint combinations. At the time there were 104 million fingerprint cards on file.

One of the fingerprint cards indicated that Elizabeth Short (known to her family and friends as Beth) was an applicant for a position as clerk in the post exchange of Camp Cooke military base in California on January 30, 1943. The other had been submitted by the Santa Barbara California Police Department, connecting her to an arrest on September 23, 1943, on charges of violating juvenile court laws, after which she was released to the probation department.

The Santa Barbara police report described her as female, Caucasian, born on July 29, 1924. Her mother, Phoebe Short, resided in Medford, Massachusetts.

The investigation in the immediate aftermath of the murder concentrated on the week leading up to the discovery of the body, and a police bulletin was circulated to officers all over the city. As well as a picture of the victim it contained information such as the fact that the fingernails were bitten to the quick and that Beth Short was last sighted at the Biltmore Hotel getting out of a car on January 9. On leaving the car she had gone into the lobby of the Biltmore.

When the history of the twenty-two-year-old was eventually revealed it showed a small-town girl who had been drawn to the bright lights of Hollywood and had dreamed of becoming a studio star. She had led a somewhat chaotic existence, a respectable female itinerant whose day-to-day existence made her dependent on and vulnerable to the opposite sex.

What transpired was that her vulnerability led her into the clutches of a homicidal sex maniac and possible serial killer, a knife-wielding Svengali who did indeed make Beth Short famous, front-page news for one of the longest periods of any murder in the United States, and the subject of at least half a dozen books, documentaries and a number of feature films.

This Hollywood dreamer became famous in death for the manner and brutality of a slaying that has haunted generations since that fateful recovery of her mutilated corpse on a vacant lot. Tinseltown was just a few miles down the road but that was as far as Beth Short got.

The path to that grisly end was not particularly happy and

if the victim's life flashed past her eyes in her last moments, she might well have thought, this earth never gave me much of a break.

At an early stage, because of her predilection for wearing black, she became known by the sobriquet the Black Dahlia. It was a strange but apt description, an ornamental flower whose leaves are often, segmented, toothed or cut.

She was born in a suburb of Boston and one year after her birth her father abandoned the family leaving her mother to bring up the family, five girls, on her own in nearby Medford. Beth was attractive and popular at the local high school but dropped out in her second year and went to work in 1942 as a waitress in Miami Beach.

There she met and apparently fell in love with an air force pilot named Major Matt Gordon Jr, who was stationed there. He was transferred overseas and they began to correspond. At one stage she sent him twenty-seven letters over an eleven-day period. In January of the following year she travelled to Santa Barbara, California where she got a job at Camp Cooke.

She left a short time afterwards and went to look for her father who she had learnt lived in a nearby area. Again her stay was brief and she returned to Santa Barbara in September 1943. Beth loved to be in the company of men in uniform. She regularly frequented clubs used by military personnel and she first came to the notice of the authorities when she was arrested in a club serving alcohol when she was only nineteen, under-age and in breach of the local liquor laws. Rather than face charges she agreed to return to Medford with a travel ticket provided by the probation service.

She led a transient existence, with no direction or focus, underlined by the fact that, despite her liking for social life, Beth Short was a loner. She had plenty of aspirations but not a lot to back them up with in the way of a plan or even a desire to settle in any one place for a decent length of time.

She continued to send letters to her overseas love and in April 1945 he, according to Beth, proposed marriage but a short time later he was killed in a plane crash in India. Her aspiration for love and marriage to an officer went down with the airman. She moved again to Miami Beach, worked as a waitress, then back to Medford and got a job as a cashier in a cinema.

Driven by what she saw on the silver screen, she moved to Hollywood in April 1946. The last nine months of her life would provide many avenues of investigation and clues, almost all of which led down blind alleys, none that led directly to the vacant lot.

Following the identification both the media and the investigation went into a frenzy of activity. LA was not short of horrible sexual murders of women and other violent homicides but this was one of the worst killings ever. It brought the level of public interest to almost hysterical proportions fuelled by the reporting and leaks from the investigation team.

The police had, like the media, to sate the public appetite and released information one day after the discovery of the body indicating that the victim was killed elsewhere and she was murdered by a sadistic killer who drove to the crime scene where the suspect's vehicle 'hurriedly stopped as evidenced by the tracks in the gutter'.

The same day, detectives interviewed police officer Myrl McBride who had information about a woman in a distressed state the night before the body was found. The policewoman positively identified Short from a photograph as the woman who had come to her sobbing in terror and whom she saw leaving a downtown bar in the company of two men and a woman.

The following day, January 17, the consulting psychiatrist for the Los Angeles Police Department, Paul De River, in a foretaste of psychological profiling told the *Los Angeles Evening Herald Express*:

> In his act, the murderer was manifesting a sadistic component of a sado-masochistic complex. These killers are usually highly perverted and resort to various forms of perversion and means of torture to satisfy their lusts.
>
> This type of suspect, above all, seeks the physical and moral pain and the disgraceful humiliation and maltreatment of his victims. These sadists have a superabundance of curiosity and are liable to spend much time with their victims after the life has flickered and died. The suspect may even be a studious type, who

delighted in feeling himself into the humiliation
of the victim. He was the experimenter and
analyst in the most brutal forms of torture.

This assessment at the time might have seemed to be a
slightly gratuitous piece of psychological nonsense but, in the
light of future decades of study of sexual psychopaths, Dr De
River might not have been too wide of the mark. Such
profiling would a couple of decades later become an essential
part of the detection kit, especially when hunting down serial
killers.

The doctor was just one part of a gigantic rush to find any
small clue that would lead to the identity of the killer or in
some way connect the perpetrator to the unfortunate victim.
Newspapers and investigating detectives competed for the
next lead and, in some instances, traded information in a most
extraordinary bartering process.

Quite often, the reporters were ahead of the investigators,
having no concept of shift work and aided by the deep
pockets of the newspaper proprietors who were willing to
shell out money to get the exclusives. Already James
Richardson had pulled off a big coup with the crime scene
report and the fingerprints. His reporters had also got the
first interview with Phoebe Short by quite cynically telling her
that her by then dead daughter had won a beauty contest. It
would not be the first time that reporters for the newspaper
would use such cruel methods of falsehood to get what they
or the news editor wanted.

The January 16 first-day edition sold more newspapers than any other edition in the history of the *Examiner*, with the exception of Victory Day of the Second World War. This murder was huge news.

Richardson's reporters had been able to locate, from a return address on a letter Beth had sent to her mother, two more witness contacts, Dorothy and Elvera French in San Diego. The Frenches, who had allowed Beth to board for free in their house for a month from December 1946 to early January 1947, told the reporters that the victim had stored a trunk at the Railway Express station in Los Angeles. They found the trunk and Richardson did a deal with Captain Donohue: he would reveal the location of the luggage in return for an *Examiner* exclusive on its contents.

Richardson described the event:

> We got the trunk but I had to call in police to get it. The company would not turn it over to a reporter. I called Jack Donohue, chief of the homicide squad.
>
> 'If I tell you where you can find the Dahlia's trunk will you agree to bring it to the *Examiner* and open it here?' I asked.
>
> 'Look, Jim,' he said. 'If I do that, every other paper in town will be after my scalp. Don't put me on the spot like that. You've caused me enough goddamn trouble the way it is with all those stories you've been breaking.'
>
> 'You want the trunk, don't you?' I said. 'No

deal, no trunk.'

Jack actually moaned. I could hear it.

'All right,' he said, 'it's a deal. I'll send a couple of boys to you. But if you were a friend of mine you'd give me a break.'

'If you're a friend of mine you'll give me a break,' I said. 'Let's be friends somehow, Jack.'

'All right, but I'm sure going to catch hell,' he said.

He told the editor that it would be the last time they would ever make a deal. Richardson was not worried knowing that as long as he had got the investigative leads in his grasp, he had leverage.

The trunk was opened in the newspaper office in the presence of reporters and detectives. The contents included many photographs of Beth Short posing with a variety of military men including a three-star general. There were also letters to Major Matt Gordon and a Lieutenant Joseph Fickling along with telegrams sent to her by a number of people. One of those, with no date, was sent to Beth Short, 220 21st Street, Miami Beach, Florida from Washington DC and read:

A promise is a promise to a person of the world.

Yours.

Enigmatic, unidentified. Was it from a suitor, a lover, the killer? There was no name and no return address and in any case what did the message mean?

But this was typical of the strange and short life of the victim of this horrible act of mutilation. Her lifestyle was chaotic, particularly in the last nine months of her nomadic existence, and she seemed to easily befriend and date men without any knowledge of their backgrounds. Dangerously, she relied on men for her meals and accommodation, mostly without sexual favour, but it did not seem to cross her mind until some short space of time before January 14 that she was in any mortal danger.

Was it naivety or part of this woman's larger flight from reality? In a town characterised equally by glamour and savagery, Beth Short could not have avoided the fact that there was a clear danger to women.

The most vulnerable section of the female population are prostitutes and while Beth Short was not a hooker by definition of the profession, she was living just a step away from the streets that the hookers patrolled.

Evidence did emerge that there was a man in her life whom Beth Short had reason to fear. There was a threatening tone to the wording of the message in the Western Union telegram from Washington DC and she had mentioned to some acquaintances that she had a boyfriend who was jealous. The state of the body of the victim, put the act well beyond any definition of a crime of passion.

Pursuing the telegram lead, LAPD investigators were sent to Miami to make enquiries in the neighbourhood in which she was living at the time, while other investigators visited people who Beth Short had been corresponding with including Lt. Fickling.

On Saturday January 18 crime reporters from the *Examiner* interviewed the Frenches in San Diego and got one step ahead in the investigation by discovering the name of a married man whom Beth Short had been dating while staying at the French household.

Dorothy French had persuaded her mother Elvera to take in Beth after she found her at a local movie theatre penniless and homeless. The Frenches told the reporters that from December 21, 1946, Beth had dated a different man every night through to the New Year.

The last time they saw Beth was on January 8, 1947, when she left with the married man, Red Manley. She packed two suitcases and she left with Red in his car.

Getting the name of the motel where Manley had stayed, the reporters checked the register and got the registration number of his car. They passed it on to city editor Richardson who then, from the California Department of Motor Vehicles, got Manley's address in the LA suburb of Huntingdon Park. Richardson sent four reporters to stake out the address. The usual deal was done between the newspaper and the LAPD but the reporters were on the spot first. Will Fowler was detailed to knock on the door with a police badge and present it in case the door was slammed in his face. A young woman, Manley's wife, answered and the reporter offered the false identification. Fowler recalled later,

A strikingly beautiful red-haired young woman

answered the front door and I flashed my Los
Angeles County Sheriff's badge without saying
that I was an officer of the law.

Manley's wife told him that Red was away on a business trip. Fowler urged her not to tell her husband that police were there which she obeyed when Red phoned. The reporter also managed to persuade her to give him a number of family portraits – some newspaper methods do not change over the ages. The posse were ready.

When Manley returned from the business trip later that day, he was ambushed by a contingent of both police and reporters. At this juncture, he was the prime suspect. LAPD detectives were not known for subtle methods of interrogation and the suspect was without doubt put under extreme pressure, including table thumping, shouting and threats but he insisted he was in no way involved with the murder. After a twelve-hour grilling he still maintained his innocence and begged to be given a lie detector test.

The first test the following day was not conclusive, a second conducted by criminalist Ray Pinker, passed him. But the apparently innocent episode with Beth would have tragic consequences for his life. And he would not be the only one.

His account of his friendship with the victim, given to police and widely reported, served to show just what a dangerous path Elizabeth Short had been going down.

Manley, a twenty-five-year-old salesman, told interrogators he had driven to San Diego about ten days before Christmas.

After doing his business calls he spotted Elizabeth Short standing on a corner across the street from the Western Airlines office. Despite the fact that his wife had just had a baby, or maybe because of it, Manley decided to engage the attractive young woman in conversation. He asked her if she wanted a lift. She resisted at first and asked him if he thought it was wrong to ask a girl at a corner whom he did not know to get into his car. She did get in and directed him to Pacific Beach where she said she was living with friends. Manley asked her out to dinner and she accepted but said that she would tell her friends that he was a colleague at Western Airlines where she said she worked.

If there was ever a weaver of a tangled web, it was Beth Short.

Manley dropped her off at the Frenches' house and booked into a nearby motel. He returned at 7 p.m. and was introduced to the Frenches. He and Beth went out for dinner and afterwards he drove back to the Frenches and sat in the car with his date. He attempted to kiss her but found that she was cold and unresponsive. He asked if he could see her again; he would wire her in advance. He then left for Los Angeles the following day.

On January 8 he returned to San Diego, called to the Western Airlines office and waited but there was no sign of Elizabeth, so he drove over to the Frenches. Beth answered the front door and asked him if he could bring her out to make a phone call. On the way she changed her mind and asked him if he would drive her to Los Angeles. He agreed but said it would have to wait until the following day as he had business to do.

They returned to the house where she packed her suitcases, bid her month-long hosts goodbye and left with Manley. He booked into a motel and they went out drinking and dancing. They got hamburgers and went back to the motel where he lit a fire as Elizabeth was complaining of feeling cold and having chills. Was this a delay tactic to put off Manley seeking sex? If so it worked, made all the easier as Manley felt guilty about his wife.

The next morning, he made his business calls, returned to pick up Elizabeth at the motel around lunchtime and drove on to Los Angeles. On the way she told him that she was meeting her sister that evening at the Biltmore Hotel. She took his address and said that she would write to him.

When they arrived in LA she asked him to drive to the Greyhound bus depot where she wanted to check in her luggage. Afterwards they drove to the Biltmore. She wanted to go to the toilet and asked him to see if her sister, Mrs West, had checked in or was in the foyer. His enquiries drew a blank. There was little doubt that this meeting was another lie.

When Elizabeth returned to the foyer, Manley left to go home. It was the last time that he ever saw her, he told the interrogators. He was questioned again and again but kept sticking to the same story. Red Manley was sorry he had ever stopped at the corner and picked up the pretty woman whose life, he now realised, was laden with deceit and danger.

Not only was he a suspect in a huge murder investigation but he was in the eye of the biggest media storm ever seen in Los Angeles, bringing shame, shock and disapproval. But, accepting that his story was true, Red Manley could be perceived to have been a very foolish man but no more; an innocent abroad compared to some of the men that the Black Dahlia had chosen for company. Men who might react entirely differently to discovering the extent of her deceit.

As the interrogators pressed him for any more detail that he could remember about their last encounter, it may not have occurred to Manley that they had changed tack and were now looking for any lead he could give them that would not end up at his door. They must have realised that at this juncture Manley was the one that had been used by the Dahlia, and others in his position might have forced sex on her and violence. One thing a sexual psychopath reacts very badly to is betrayal and rejection by a woman. Red Manley did not fit into that category.

Under the harsh lights of the room, with the interrogators just shadows in the background, Red Manley began going over in his mind again and again the events of January 8. There were details that he might not have wanted to recall even though they did not implicate him. He was run ragged now by the unrelenting questioning and he might just as well give every detail however incriminating it might seem to his interrogators.

He remembered seeing scratches on both of Elizabeth's arms on the outside and above the elbows. He was not a violent man, they had nothing to do with him. He swore that he had never committed any violent act towards her, he was just looking for a bit of diversion, typical of the travelling business type. He did not want this to be death of a salesman. He told them that Beth said she had a very jealous boyfriend, describing him as Italian looking with very dark hair.

Red Manley was drowning in the meaningless conversational detail of the time but he had to go on. He knew that he was going to sink right to the bottom, dragged down by his stupid inclination to engage with Beth Short. It was disastrous at this moment, though it had not seemed so stupid then. He could have kept driving, why hadn't he? It all seemed trivial then, all so horrible now. His interrogators were putting him through every second of every hour with a woman he barely knew. He could see his young life already ruined by a chance encounter. But he had to go on. He had no choice.

He now remembered that Elizabeth had indeed made a long-distance call on January 8 from a café just outside San Diego to a man in Los Angeles. He overheard enough of the call to deduce that she had arranged to meet this man the following evening, January 9.

Though he did not know it, Manley's mention of the injuries held a resonance for the investigators whose colleagues had received information from a taxi driver. Apparently during her stay with the Frenches, Elizabeth had gone to Los Angeles for a few days over the Christmas. Glen Chanslor the taxi driver identified a woman whom he had driven downtown to a hotel as Elizabeth.

He said that at 7.30 p.m. on December 29, she had run to his stand seeking help after she claimed a man had assaulted her. She was wild-eyed, hysterical and bleeding from her knees. Her clothing was torn and her shoes were missing. She told him that she had been driven to the stand by some strangers who had picked her up.

She explained her predicament by saying that a well-dressed man whom she knew and worked with had offered to take her to Long Beach so she could cash her weekly paycheck. Instead, he had driven her down a lonely road, parked the car and attacked her.

Chanslor drove her to the hotel where she was staying downtown. He waited while she went to her room to fix herself up. When she returned she told him that she did not have the fare. She had not shown him a paycheck as evidence of her story, or promised to pay him again. He just put it down as a loss and drove off.

His story broadly corroborated Manley's about the injuries he had observed on January 8. Her explanation of how her injuries were sustained is dubious. It is far more likely that she met this man in the same way that she first encountered Manley but this man whose car she had got into was far less tolerant of sexual rejection than the salesman.

The following Monday Mr and Mrs William Johnson, owners of the East Washington Boulevard Hotel, told investigators and, inevitably, reporters that Elizabeth Short and a man claiming to be her husband booked a room on

Sunday, January 12 registering under the name of Mr and Mrs Barnes. They then disappeared, the man returning to the hotel three days later in a state of nervousness and agitation. Mr Johnson told him that as he and Mrs Barnes had not been seen for three days he thought they were dead. The man, visibly shaken, immediately left the hotel. The Johnsons identified Elizabeth Short from photographs as Mrs Barnes. The investigators were given a detailed description of the man, but this for some strange reason was never publicly released.

On January 23 ace crime reporter Agnes Underwood, writing in the *Herald Express*, connected the Dahlia murder with other unsolved slayings in the city and speculated that it, like the others, including Ora Murray, Georgette Bauerdorf and Gertrude Evelyn Landon, might remain unsolved. Underwood's article, typical of those at the time, started under a heading:

WEREWOLVES LEAVE TRAIL OF WOMEN MURDERS IN LA

In the gory album of unsolved murders, kidnappings and crimes against women in general, Los Angeles police may have to insert a new page: The Mystery of the Sadistic Slaying of Elizabeth Short, the Black Dahlia. So far, all clues have failed. This latest murder mystery which has provoked the greatest mobilisation of crime detection experts in the city's history, is the latest in a long series. The finding of her dismembered body was preceded by other gruesome discoveries of women victims, slain for lust, for revenge, for reasons unknown.

The article provided names of seven recent lone victims of sex-related murders, all unsolved. It seemed that, long before the manifestation of the Ted Bundys, Silence of the Lambs, and other monster murderers, in Los Angeles of the forties there was a serial killer on the loose.

But of course Jack the Ripper had committed a series of similarly unsolved mutilations on prostitutes in Victorian London. Over the generations, the similarities were evident, most especially in this case where the perpetrator was speculated to have medical knowledge to enable the murder of Short.

He would also ape his predecessor by sending messages to newspapers and the investigation team. As with Jack the Ripper, and subsequent serial-killer experience indicates, the perpetrators have a propensity to connect with the investigation team.

The findings of medical examiner Dr Frederic Newbarr in his autopsy report, some of which were kept secret to flush out crackpot confessors to the murder, served to expand the horror of the death of the victim. He stated in his report that he had performed an autopsy on Elizabeth Short on January 16, 1947, at the Los Angeles County Coroner's mortuary and found that the immediate cause of death was haemorrhage and shock due to concussion of the brain and lacerations of the face. This is an edited version of his report:

> The body is that of a female of about fifteen to twenty years of age, measuring 5'5" in height and weighing 115 lbs. There are multiple lacerations to the mid-forehead and the right forehead and the top of the head. There are multiple tiny abrasions, linear in shape, on the right face and forehead. There are two small lacerations on each side of the nose near the bridge. There is a deep laceration on the face three inches long which extends laterally from the right corner of the mouth. There is a deep laceration two and one half inches long extending from the left corner of the mouth. The surrounding tissues are bluish purple in colour. There are five linear lacerations in the right upper lip. The teeth are in a state of advanced decay. The two upper central incisors are loose, and one lower incisor is loose. The rest of the teeth show cavities.
>
> On the scalp there is ecchymosis [bruising due to seeping blood in wounded tissue] in the right and upper frontal area. There are localised areas of subarachnoid haemorrhage on the right side and small haemorrhagic areas in the corpus callosum. No fracture of the skull is visible.
>
> There is a depressed ridge on both sides and

in the anterior portion of the neck. There are
two linear abrasions in the left anterior neck.
There are two depressed ridges in the posterior
neck. The lower ridge has an abrasion in the skin
at each extremity.

There is an irregular laceration with superficial
tissue loss in the skin of the right breast. The
tissue loss is more or less square in outline.

Dr Newbarr noted other cuts on the skin of the lower chest
and close to the nipple on the left breast and the right
forearm. He observed the fact that the fingernails were very
short. He then came to the most horrific injuries.

The trunk is completely severed by an incision
which is almost straight through the abdomen,
severing the intestine and soft tissue, passing
through the invertebral disk between the second
and third lumbar vertebrae. There is a gaping
laceration from the umbilicus to the suprapubic
region. There are multiple criss-cross
lacerations in the pubic area which extend
through the skin and soft tissues.

He noted more lacerations to the right hip, and that the
organs of the abdomen were entirely exposed. He also
recovered a piece of lacerated skin which had been cut from
the victim and put in the vagina and there was evidence that
the anus had been attacked with an object. Pubic hair had

been shaved away and inserted in the anus. The medical examiner also discovered faeces in the stomach.

He also noted, but which was only later exposed in John Gilmore's excellent book *Severed*, written after twenty-three years of researching the case, that Beth Short had an undeveloped vaginal canal, suggesting that she was incapable of normal sexual intercourse. This fact would have had a direct impact on the nature of the killer's mutilation of the body.

As in all postmortem reports, Dr Newbarr presented the facts without interpretation or comment. But even in the cold prose of science what is described is a death almost beyond belief, with mutilation and perverted acts that rivalled the worst of Jack the Ripper's killings. There was nothing disorganised or panic-driven about the killing; it was deliberate and sadistic, and the victim was subjected to appalling pain and degradation. The bisected body had been drained of blood and washed clean, probably in a bath, then brought to the location where it was found and deliberately posed to impose further postmortem humiliation.

The investigators must have pored over the possible scenario of this gruesome killing. Given the lack of defensive injuries on the body, it was highly likely that the victim had been restrained to allow the torture to have taken place.

The multiple lacerations to the various parts of Beth's body were carried out while the victim was alive as a form of torture presumably to allow the killer complete domination over the victim and to savour her terror. The cuts from each side of the mouth to the ears were also carried out while the victim was alive, as evidenced by the presence of blood seeping through the wounded tissue.

The faeces could not have been ingested if the victim was already unconscious or dead. In other words, it was forced down her mouth and throat while she was still alive. This would possibly have been from the insertion of faeces-stained underwear into her mouth, or a faeces-stained penis after anal rape. There was no way for the medical examiner to determine where the faeces originated from – the victim or the perpetrator.

The bisection did happen after the victim was dead and most likely was executed in a bath, as disposal of the blood in any other way would have left large blood stains which would have been virtually impossible to conceal.

A perpetrator with medical knowledge or experience could have carried out this process with the sort of ease that would leave little blood evidence, particularly if the huge volume of blood was drained efficiently down the plughole of a sizeable bath. For that to happen the bisected parts of the body would have to have been hung like carcasses in an abattoir.

The highly efficient bisection of the body and the retention of the organs which were found in the body at the site of the disposal indicated the killer had medical knowledge. Without such medical or anatomical knowledge a killer would have left a murder site of physical destruction that would have been almost impossible to manage.

This begs the question why medical professionals were not targeted at an early stage of the investigation. Perhaps the top echelons of Los Angeles society and the authorities could not afford to handle this potential can of worms. Los Angeles, like any other city in a boom, was a hotbed of corruption, and with that comes depravity and the necessity to cover up. In such an atmosphere anyone anywhere can be bought, and silence brings huge premiums.

There is little doubt that *Los Angeles Examiner* city editor James Richardson, given the level of cooperation with the investigation team, had more than a good idea of what the autopsy report contained but would keep the more gory details to himself to allow the investigators deal with the possibility of false confessions. Another telling example of that bond is the fact that crime scene photographs of the body never came into the public domain until four decades after the murder. Richardson also knew that Beth Short had an undeveloped vaginal canal. There was further information that the newsman would keep to himself to preserve his good relationship with the LAPD.

On the afternoon of January 23 Richardson received a phone call – from a man identifying himself as the Black Dahlia killer.

The man congratulated the editor on the *Examiner's* handling of the case but noted that the paper had run out of material. Richardson agreed it had. The man said he could offer assistance, a phrase that sent shivers up the editor's spine. Richardson wrote a note and passed it to his assistant: Trace this call. The man offered to send Richardson items belonging to the Black Dahlia but then cut short the call recognising that Richardson would be trying to have it traced.

The following day, after a tip-off, investigators learnt that the suspect had left Short's purse and shoes on top of a trashcan in front of a motel, twenty blocks away from where the body was discovered. Meantime, the trashcan had been collected and brought to the city dump. After a long search the purse and shoes were located. Red Manley positively identified the shoes.

The killer was not averse to leaving clues or indeed taunting the investigation team and the media, no matter what the risks involved. And he kept his promise to Richardson.

The *Examiner* was sent by mail dated January 24 (but intercepted by postal inspectors), a package containing some of the victim's belongings, including identification, address book, birth certificate and security card. Also included was a note made from letters cut from newspapers, which read:

Here is Dahlia's belongings. Letter to follow.

The package had been soaked or washed with petrol in an attempt to wipe out fingerprints. Fingerprints were found on the package and sent to the FBI for examination. Newspapers reported that the prints were clear. They omitted to inform their readers that the package had been handled by quite a few people with nothing to do with the murder. The FBI noted that most if not all of the fingerprints were from the handlers. This parcel full of items belonging to the victim had promised much but led nowhere.

The address book contained seventy-five names but one page, possibly containing the killer's name, had been torn out. On the cover, embossed in gold lettering, was the name Mark Hansen. Hansen was part owner of a club called the Florentine Gardens, a popular nightspot in LA which attracted politicians, the rich and famous and, naturally, top underworld figures who were not at all averse to mixing with each other. In this post-war boom in LA, the top guys had relationships for their mutual benefit. There were also the chorus girls who worked in the club, all wanting to enter into the Hollywood fold. Some would make it, most would not. Elizabeth Short did not.

Hansen lived behind the club and often rented rooms to the girls. He was questioned by investigators following the seizure of the package and admitted that he had rented a room to the victim for a month in the summer of 1946 and said that she had dated many men during that period. He identified the leather address book and claimed that it had been stolen from his desk. He said that had happened shortly before Elizabeth Short moved out. He claimed that, contrary to newspaper reports, he had never dated or had any relationship with the victim. The last time he had seen her was at Christmas, three weeks before her murder.

The investigators found no reason to disbelieve Hansen's statement.

On January 27, a Monday, another message, on a postcard and apparently from the killer, was addressed to the *Examiner*. It read:

Here it is
Turning in Wed
January 29 10 a.m.
Had my fun at police
Black Dahlia Avenger

Captain Donohue said in a statement the fact that the killer had written his message as opposed to using cut-out lettering indicated that he intended to turn himself in. He had taken no precaution to conceal his identity by writing it by hand and Donohue invited him to meet at any public location or at the homicide office in City Hall.

Analysis of the postcard revealed the use of a ballpoint pen, a rarity in 1947 and, at a cost of twelve dollars, was used almost exclusively by professionals, including lawyers and medical professionals.

The next communication used pasted lettering and said

Dahlia's Killer Cracking
Wants Terms.

And:

I will give up in
Dahlia killing if I get
10 years
Don't try to find me

LAPD crime lab analysed the envelopes and the paper used, which indicated that they had all come from the same source as the original package. There were several dark hairs embedded in the tape used to stick on the words but did not match with the victim's.

A fifth note was intercepted by the LAPD at the Terminal Annexe Post Office. It was scribbled on glossy paper torn from a notepad and read:

> A certain girl is going to get the same as E.S.
> got if she squeals on us.
> We're going to Mexico City – catch us if you
> can.
> 2 K's

On the reverse of the mailed envelope the sender wrote:

> E. Short got it. Caral Marshall is next.

The *Examiner* enlisted leading forensic handwriting expert Clark Sellers to analyse the hand printing on the postcards. He said that it was evident the writer had taken great pains to disguise his or her personality by printing instead of writing the message, and by endeavouring to appear illiterate. But the style and formation of the printed letters betrayed the writer as an educated person.

Not an original summation: it echoed precisely the analysis of the messages sent by Jack the Ripper. Perhaps the sender had more than a passing knowledge of the murders in the Whitechapel area of London and the taunting messages sent to the newspapers and the police there.

Another pasted note was sent to Captain Donohue, saying

that the killer had changed his mind and was not giving himself up and that the killing was justified. Six additional messages were published in *The Herald Express*, purporting to come from the killer.

Author John Gilmore was convinced that all the messages sent to the police and newspapers, including the package with the victim's personal effects, were actually manufactured by the media to keep the story in the headlines.

The notes, genuine or not, kept the headlines afloat and the public appetite for the case temporarily satisfied but, as the investigators well knew, the more time that went by there was increasingly less likelihood that the killer would be caught. The newspapers got 'expert assessments' from well-known writers of fictional crime whose conclusions could only be regarded, at best, as highly speculative. All stuck to the party line that the killer would be soon behind bars. *The Herald Express* called in Leslie Charteris, creator of *The Saint* series of books. His was one of the better and more credible contributions where he proposed the killer was impotent:

> Whether the murderer's impotence was or was not due to alcohol, and whether his resulting rage was or was not inflamed by the same thing, I can see him saying something like, 'So you think you can laugh at me do you? I'll keep that laugh on your face for good,' and he slashes her cheeks from the corners of her mouth to her ears, in the ghostly grin which is preserved in

the morgue photos.

I am practically certain that the man will be caught and I base this on a rather gruesome reason. My reason is that, even if he should get away with this murder, it is almost certain that he will repeat it, and the next time he does he has another chance to make a slip.

Meanwhile there was a sensational confession by an army corporal, Joseph Dumais. Despite the fact that it could not have been credible in any way since four of his colleagues testified that he was in Fort Dix, New Jersey at the time of the murder, police and the media gave it plenty of coverage.

The hoax sparked the theory that if there was a false confessor the real killer would turn himself in to expose the false confession. A more likely outcome, however, would be that he would kill again to prove his credentials and expose the irresponsibility of the police and media in foisting an impostor on the public.

It was less the fault of the police who had to pursue every lead however unpromising, but the investigation authorities did little to stem the hysterical media tide that proclaimed in a February 8 *Herald Express* screaming front-page headline:

CORPORAL DUMAIS IS
BLACK DAHLIA KILLER

Two days later it was less sensationally revealed that Dumais was not in fact the killer. In the interim, however, there had been another murder – which seemed to carry the real Dahlia killer's signature.

In the early morning of Monday, February 10, just over three weeks after the Black Dahlia killing, another gruesome discovery was made on another vacant lot, seven miles from the Short murder scene. Another nude female body was found by a construction worker at around 8 a.m. in the morning. The corpse was a bloody mess, bludgeoned and lacerated, involving a huge amount of gratuituous as well as calculated violence.

Detectives examining the scene and the body noted foot and heel marks on the victim's face, breast and hands, and other disturbing hallmarks including messages written in red lipstick on the torso of the victim. There was an obscenity, later revealed as FUCK YOU, scrawled and then the letters B.D. – a blatant reference to the murder of Short.

Near the body the victim's purse and a lipstick container were found. The victim's stockings and underwear were missing but her coat and her dress were draped over the body. Her shoes were arranged near her head. A man's white handkerchief and an empty wine bottle were also found at the scene.

A crime scene photographer took close-ups of the lipstick handwriting and technical officers took plaster cast impressions of footprints. The examination was much more meticulous than that carried out at the Short scene. Black hair follicles were found under the fingernails of the victim which indicated that the woman had put up a struggle.

There was a large pool of blood found on the highway near the scene which indicated to investigators that the killer, or killers, had dragged the body to the vacant lot before posing the body and writing the messages on the torso.

As in the Dahlia case, the killer was able to combine sadistic violence with cool calculation in the aftermath and a high degree of risk-taking in the moving and placing of the victim. Those traits did not necessarily mean that the same killer was responsible for both murders but there were enough similarities to make comparisons.

The victim was identified as Jeanne French a woman who, a decade before, had achieved more fame than Elizabeth Short had hoped for as a socialite and wannabe Hollywood star. She had worked as a contract star, registered as a nurse and got a pilot's licence. She became known as the Flying Nurse.

Jeanne French seemed to be destined for great things in whatever she chose to do but when she married she seemed to let go of all her ambitions. In the twenties she was a travelling companion to famed oil heiress Millicent Rogers and also a nurse to Marion Wilson, who turned up each year on the anniversary of Rudolph Valentino's death as the mysterious veiled woman who placed flowers on his grave.

It seemed unimaginable that Jeanne French would share the same fate as the Black Dahlia, who ironically and posthumously became far more famous than the victim of the red lipstick murder.

Dr Frederic Newbarr carried out the postmortem examination. French's ribs had been shattered by heavy blows, and one of the broken ribs had pierced her heart, causing haemorrage and death. The contents of her stomach were examined and the pathologist concluded that she had eaten chop suey within an hour of her death which determined that she had been murdered on the same day sometime between midnight and 4 a.m.

Toxicology tests also found a high level of alcohol in the victim's bloodstream. In other words, in the evening leading up to her death, Jeanne French had, as the phrase goes, been out on the town. And maybe being in that state she had not chosen her company too carefully. No more than Beth Short had done.

In the immediate aftermath the investigation team, having established the identity of the victim, began to put together the last movements of Jeanne French in an attempt to establish a connection with her brutal killer.

It was soon known that on the previous night, Sunday, at around 7.30 p.m. she had gone to the Plantation Café on Washington Boulevard in Los Angeles in the company of two men. One man was described by a waitress as having dark hair and a small moustache. She told investigators that the two men had gone to the booth while French made a call from a phone in the restaurant. It was a long call, lasting ten minutes.

The waitress noticed that the two men were arguing, her interpretation being that the argument revolved around which one was going to go with the woman who was still on the phone. After they had eaten, the men left, followed shortly by Jeanne French.

Later that evening she was seen at the wheel of her 1928 Ford Roadster driving away from her home and less than half an hour later she was witnessed in another restaurant on Santa Monica Boulevard in an intoxicated state. An hour later she was in a nearby bar where she told a bartender that she was going to have her husband committed to a psychiatric ward.

Jeanne French was on a high roll that night, which could have ended up like many a drunken night for most people, back at home and nursing a bad hangover the following day. Apparently there was some substance in her drunken threats to have her husband put away: some time before they had had a bad row, he had moved out and divorce proceedings were in the offing. Later that night she had in fact visited her husband, Frank, at his apartment and told him to be in her lawyer's office the next morning as she was filing for divorce. By now, well intoxicated, she argued with him before driving away and arriving at a drive-in restaurant shortly before midnight where she had the chop suey in the company of a dark-haired man with a small moustache. Her car was still in the restaurant parking lot at 2 a.m. It was concluded that she had left with this man.

Her husband was quickly eliminated as a suspect despite their marital problems; there was nothing to connect him with either the opportunity or the crime scene. The killer, whether connected to the Black Dahlia murder or not, was on

Murder victim Sarah Payne.

Convicted murderer, Roy Whiting.

Extensive blood-staining outside the patio door on OJ Simpson's property.

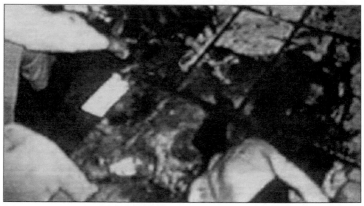

Nicole Simpson lies in a pool of her own blood. Blood droplets on her back could only have come from her attacker, crucial evidence which was ignored and then washed away.

Assistant State Pathologist Dr Declan Gilsenan.

The body of a woman is removed from a house in which she was murdered. Crime scenes like this where relatives and friends may have had a lot of prior access pose particular problems for investigators. *(Collins Photo Agency)*

Elizabeth Short –
The Black Dahlia

The bisected body of the Black Dahlia dumped on a waste lot in
Los Angeles.

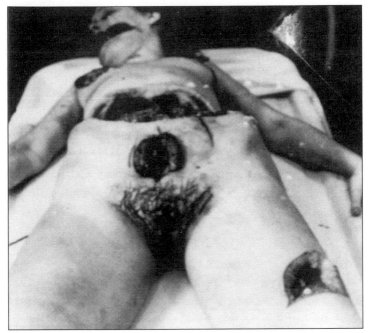

Elizabeth Short's body on the morgue table. There are large knife gouges in the lower stomach and left leg.

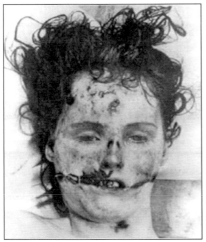

Elizabeth Short's once beautiful face has been extensively mutilated by the killer.

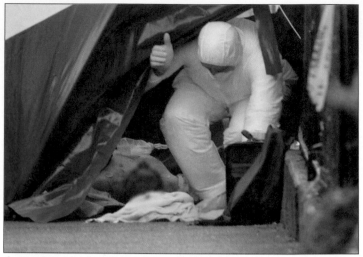

A member of a forensic team exits a tent containing the body of a murder victim. *(Collins Photo Agency)*

A forensic expert examines the scene around the covered body of a victim of a gangland assassination. *(Collins Photo Agency)*

Murder victim Siobhán Hynes. *(Collins Photo Agency)*

John McDonagh convicted of murder. *(Collins Photo Agency)*

JonBenet on stage in a pageant queen competition.

Patsy and John Ramsey

JonBenet Ramsey in one of her pageant queen poses.

An investigator enters the Ramsey crime scene

JonBenet Ramsey's headstone

Blood spatter at the scene of a Dublin gangland murder.
(Collins Photo Agency)

A bullet hole in a window at the same scene.
(Collins Photo Agency)

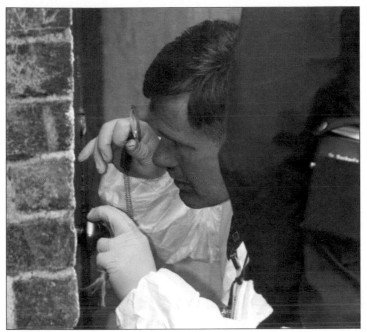

A Garda fingerprint expert examines fingerprints on the door of a house at a crime scene. *(Collins Photo Agency)*

Rachel O'Reilly was a beautiful and fit young mother with her life ahead of her.

Rachel O'Reilly's body is removed from the house by members of
the forensic and technical team. *(Collins Photo Agency)*

Investigators search for the murder weapon near the scene of the
Rachel O'Reilly murder. Believed to be a barbell, it has never
been found. *(Collins Photo Agency)*

State Pathologist Marie Cassidy arrives at a crime scene.
(Collins Photo Agency)

A walk led Rachel Kiely into the path of a sexual predator.
(Collins Photo Agency)

Ian Horgan was convicted of the manslaughter of Rachel Kiely.
(Collins Photo Agency)

Crime scene veteran: former State Pathologist Dr John Harbison.
(Collins Photo Agency)

David Lawler used the Internet to check the forensic implications of rape and murder. However he did not make allowances for cold climatic conditions which helped preserve his semen sample and secure a conviction for the rape and murder of Marilyn Rynn. *(Collins Photo Agency)*

DNA fingerprint pioneer, Sir Alec Jeffreys.

Colin Pitchfork – the first murderer caught and convicted by DNA fingerprinting.

the loose and, as it transpired, would never be caught.

From subsequent experience, it has been proven again and again that random killers are more easily tracked down, while serial killers are only apprehended after a long period of time and a trail of human destruction. And more often than not deliver themselves by simple mistakes born of complacency.

A possible connection between the two murders seemed to pose a problem for the top authorities in the LAPD. Captain Donohue, who was of the opinion that there was a connection, was soon after removed as officer in charge of the two investigations and transferred from the homicide division to head of the robbery division. That could have been routine police policy, replacing him with a fresh face, but other interpretations down the years would see this more in the light of a cover-up.

After years researching the case, author John Gilmore in his book *Severed* claimed not only to have identified the killer but to have met him on a number of occasions. He reported the man to the LAPD. They were about to move on the case when the man died in a fire in a seedy hotel, possibly started by one of his own cigarettes, in 1982, three and a half decades after the murder.

Gilmore named the killer as an alcoholic drifter by the name of Jack Anderson Wilson who also went by the name of Arnold Smith. The man, whom he met in a number of dingy bars in LA and who was always in need of a drink and a smoke, showed Gilmore a photograph of a body which the author recognised from crime scene and postmortem photographs as that of Beth Short. The only problem was the head had been cut off the photograph leaving a question mark over the true identity. Wilson did impart knowledge of the murder and the mutilation of the victim that only the killer could have known but blamed another man for the actual killing.

While the authorities were willing to move on the information provided by Gilmore, there was little point when the suspect died, and as the author put it, the nightmare scenario played itself out. For a writer who had spent over two decades investigating the murder, the possibility of a solution was taken away cruelly right before the finishing tape.

Asked to explain his motivation for spending so much time on it, to his personal and financial detriment, he gave a simple answer that went to the heart of the brutal murder of Elizabeth Short:

> The pale white body, severed in two and left for
> the world to view; and her name, Black Dahlia.

As convincing a book that *Severed* is, the conclusion is a question rather than an answer.

Former LAPD murder detective Steve Hodel takes an even greater leap in his book *Black Dahlia Avenger* in which he names his father Dr George Hodel, a prominent physician at the time, as being the killer not only of the Black Dahlia and Jeanne French but also of other women in the city.

After his father died at the age of ninety-one, Hodel found

a photograph album among the old man's effects which included two pictures of the Black Dahlia, one with her eyes closed in an uncanny preview of her death. Hodel outlines the degenerate lifestyle of his father who participated in orgies in the family home – not a great distance from where the body of Beth Short was found – and was also tried but acquitted of having incestuous relations with his fourteen-year-old daughter. George Hodel was also involved in an abortion ring. Like the good detective he was, Steve Hodel assembled a mass of evidence implicating his father, backed up by the fact that the killer had surgical expertise. Steve Hodel provides motive and opportunity and a frightening portrait of his father as a psychopathic monster.

What Steve Hodel had in common with John Gilmore despite their difference about the identity of the killer was the denigration as well as the subordination of truth and investigative facts following the publication of their books. Despite highly interesting and controversial findings of the authors, both were rubbished by *Los Angeles Times* in-house expert, Larry Harnisch, while official LAPD sources said nothing. When Hodel did get a look at the Dahlia files courtesy of District Attorney Steve Cooley, they confirmed that his father was indeed a prime suspect in the Short and French murders and in other killings of the time.

The files further substantiated both writers' contention that between 1947 and 1950 the LAPD obstructed justice, sanitised files, and perpetuated a cover-up of the facts – a cover up which, Hodel and Gilmore claim, continues to this day. Why this should have happened can only be speculated upon and must be placed in the context of the atmosphere of corruption that existed in the city, most graphically expressed in James Ellroy's *LA Confidential* – fact masquerading brilliantly as fiction.

Under a weather-beaten pink marble stone in Oakland's Mountain View Cemetery the Black Dahlia lies with the simple inscription:

> DAUGHTER, ELIZABETH SHORT
> July 29, 1924 – January 15, 1947.

All the main characters who played a part in this tragic tale now lie under headstones, including the killer, all now silent, their dreams and ambitions, like those of the victim, consigned to the company of the dust from whence they came, scattered in clay. Resting in peace? Who knows.

In the beginning there was the severed body of Beth Short found on the vacant lot on the morning of January 15, 1947, and in the end, a continuing legacy of shadows from that horrendous discovery and, of course, the mystery. The unending mystery.

10

SAVAGE MURDER IN GALWAY

Murder no knows no bounds or borders and killers will go to great lengths to hide and disguise their evil deeds. They operate in the knowledge that the forces of law and order have to prove in a court of law that they committed these deeds and must satisfy a jury that they committed the crimes beyond all reasonable doubt.

Killers may act with brutality and savagery beyond all reason but investigators have to bring supreme logic and reason to the task of successfully prosecuting the criminals, and in the most time-consuming and painstaking fashion. The modus operandi of detection must be beyond reproach.

Investigators cannot put a foot wrong or the case could fall apart and, unlike the killers, are bound by rigorous procedures at every stage of the investigation, arrest, charging and bringing to justice of the perpetrators.

These procedures, however well set out, must adapt to the individual demands of the case. No two murders are the same. Methods and motivation vary, some are planned and others are random. Most are carried out with a brutality that ordinary law-abiding citizens have great difficulty in comprehending. Understanding the mindset of cruel killers who deliberately set out to wreak such destruction on another human being that it takes away the most precious gift that has been given to us – life itself – is also an impossibility.

Even the smallest and most close-knit communities are subject to the horrifying fallout of murder as the following case of savage murder in rural County Galway illustrates.

On the evening of December 5, 1998, teenager Siobhán Hynes started her Saturday night out in Plunkett's bar in Leitir Mór in the Galway Gaeltacht with her sister, Áine. At around midnight, they decided to travel with two friends to a GAA social that was taking place a few miles away in the popular village of Carraroe. Although Siobhán was from the village of Scones ten miles away, she attended school in Carraroe. She was recognised by bouncers outside Josie's nightclub who, observing the licensing laws, had to refuse the young girl entry. While Áine went into the club with her friend Rachel Flaherty, Siobhán decided to sit in the car listening to music with John Paul Connolly and Michael Coyne.

Not far away gardaí were keeping a discreet eye on a local man by the name of John McDonagh. Known by the nickname of 'Demesne', several local people had seen him earlier in the evening rowing in public with his former girlfriend and mother of his child, and her new boyfriend. During the argument, McDonagh had struck her on the head and then assaulted her boyfriend. The gardaí were notified and they went to the scene. They issued a warning to

McDonagh and kept him in their sights in the aftermath.

In a later statement to gardaí, nineteen-year-old John Paul Connolly recalled in detail the events of that fateful night.

> Áine and Rachel went into Josie's nightclub, while Michael Coyne, Siobhán and I remained in the car listening to tapes. We were there about five minutes when Fergus Joyce drove past and blew the hooter. Michael got out and headed towards Fergus's car. He told us that he would be back in a minute, but we knew from previous occasions that he would be back in half an hour.
>
> Siobhán remained in the front seat, while I lay in the back seat. We just continued listening to tapes. We could see the patrol car parked at Josie's. One garda was inside the door of Josie's while the other was in the patrol car.
>
> I saw a fellow sitting on the wall near our car. He was a big blondie fellow in his early twenties. He was wearing a white T-shirt and had blond hair, cut short. He did not appear to be drunk.
>
> At around 12.30 a.m., Siobhán said that she needed to go to the bathroom. I told her to go to Josie's, however she said that she would run down to a local bar. She came back a minute later and said that the doorman refused to let her into the premises.
>
> On her way back to the car she spoke to the

big blond fellow. She told me he said he was involved in some sort of trouble and he was going to beat up the two gardaí. She said his name was John 'Demesne' McDonagh and that he was not a nice guy. She then mentioned something about his girlfriend.

I did not know John McDonagh before that, but after Siobhán sat back into the car, he walked by three times. I can remember him looking into the car as he passed on one occasion. He seemed to walk past the car, sit on the wall and then back again. I can remember saying to Siobhán he was a weirdo.

At about 12.40 Siobhán said she needed to find a bathroom. I told her to go to An Feadóg chip shop as I was aware there were toilets there. Siobhán left the car and headed in the direction of An Feadóg. I did not see a person sitting on the wall at this stage. After she crossed the road I lay back in the back seat and did not see her after that.

Michael Coyne arrived back after five minutes. He asked where Siobhán was and I told him that she had gone to An Feadóg chip shop. Michael thought this strange as he had not seen her on the road on his way back. We talked in the car for about five minutes before driving slowly in the direction of An Feadóg. I went in and asked

the woman who worked there if she had seen
Siobhán. She said she had not seen her and that
she had not called there at any stage during the
night.

We were looking around for her when we met
John Coyne and Fergus Joyce. I asked them if
they had seen Siobhán and they said they had
not. We drove around Carraroe for ten minutes
looking for Siobhán.

The two young men then returned to the chipper and asked
a number of people if they had seen her and everyone replied
in the negative. They checked a number of other locations
including the hackney office but to no avail. At about
1.40 a.m. they decided to go home, slightly worried but not
alarmed by the fact that Siobhán did not turn up; she could
have bumped into her sister or friends and made her way
home with them.

As it transpired, she never arrived home.

The following morning John Paul Connolly received a
phone call around 11.30 a.m. from Mrs Coyne enquiring
whether Siobhán was with him. She said that Siobhán's
mother had been in contact with her and was worried about
the fact that Siobhán had not arrived home. John Paul could
offer no explanation and immediately made his way to
Plunkett's bar where he met a friend, Sorcha Keedy. They got
a hackney cab to Carraroe and searched for the missing girl.

Some time before, Carraroe resident Tommy Kelly was

hunting in the fields with his two dogs and eventually made his way to Tismeán beach. The dogs ran on ahead. He noticed they were lingering and behaving oddly near the seaweed-coated rocks. Wondering what had attracted their attention he went over to investigate the source of his dogs' attention. As he got close to the rocks he saw the body of a young girl lying face downwards, leaning towards her right side and with her feet pointing towards the sea.

At first he thought she might just be sleeping off the aftermath of a night out. As he leant down near her head he noticed blood seeping from her nose. He asked her was she all right. There was no reply, and then it struck him like a thunderbolt – the girl was dead. He ran back to his house, his dogs now trailing him and rang the police and the ambulance.

The body on the rocks by the sea was quickly identified as that of Siobhán Hynes.

Meanwhile, John Paul Connolly and his friends were still searching for the lost teenager who just one week before had celebrated her seventeenth birthday.

> We continued to search until we heard she had been found at Tismeán beach. We went down to the beach and we saw her body in a blanket on the rocks.
>
> To my knowledge Siobhán would never get into a car with a stranger. I just can't understand what happened. She just left and said that she would be back in ten minutes and disappeared.

The young man had, less than a day before, shared time and pleasantries in the car with a young girl who had everything in life to look forward to – finding a career, falling in love, getting married, having children. And now she was gone and all that was gone. Her friends and the community were plunged into a chasm of shock, disbelief and revulsion.

A full-scale murder investigation was started and Assistant State Pathologist Marie Cassidy made her way from Dublin to the scene of the crime. After a preliminary examination at the scene and when the crime scene technical examination had been completed, the body was removed to hospital in Galway where a full postmortem took place.

Professor Cassidy established that the immediate cause of death was due to drowning. While a substantial amount of sea water was found in her lungs, the postmortem revealed that the victim had suffered horribly before death.

The pathologist noted severe injuries to the vagina as well as to the anal area and the breasts. Although there was mottled bruising of the scalp, the skull was still intact. There were injuries to the neck, including bruising to the muscles and a fracture of the larynx. These injuries suggested that Siobhán was grabbed with enough violence and strength to strangle her but was released before that point.

Scratch marks were found on her hips and the injuries to her vagina were established to have been caused by the insertion of some object or implement which was not present at the scene of the crime.

It was hard for even seasoned members of the Garda

investigation team to believe that there was a monster living in the quiet and peaceful community capable of such a perverted murder of an innocent teenage girl, loved by her family and friends, and beloved of the area. Their first thoughts on the identity of the killer were that he must have been a stranger and that the killing was random and opportunistic.

However, operating on the well-accepted fact that the majority of murder victims either know or have had some contact with the perpetrator, the focus of the investigation would begin in Carraroe. They combed the area close to the beach and Garda divers searched the sea. A number of items and clues were unearthed. Some money, cosmetics and a hair grip belonging to the victim were recovered from the sea while her jacket was discovered not far from where the body was found.

The jacket was of particular significance because if there was a struggle there could be fibre or other forensic evidence left by the killer. Further back towards the hinterland, underwear belonging to the victim was recovered. It was clear to the investigators that the attack had taken place around this area and then the body had been brought to the seashore in the hope that the tide would take the body out to sea.

It also appeared to investigators that the killer had first removed the victim's clothes and then crudely replaced what he could find in the darkness to give the impression, had the body been washed out to sea, of suicide. It was a foolish notion and ill thought out, for a cursory investigation would have established that Siobhán Hynes was a bright, lively and loving girl without a spot of darkness on her optimistic horizon.

Every investigation team casts the net of suspicion wide at first and then narrows down the focus as those with the potential to have been involved in the crime are eliminated. Gardaí traced the movements of each suspect on the evening of Saturday December 5.

Given the fact that he had walked by the car in which the victim was sitting with her friend, and his propensity for violence, John McDonagh was high on the list of suspects. When his movements were put together it emerged that he had consumed a large quantity of alcohol that day while visiting a number of pubs. Shop CCTV cameras also established the exact items of clothing worn by him on the day.

As the investigation team sharpened its focus, Siobhán's funeral saw hundreds of mourners from the community, united in grief, at the poignant ceremony. Parish priest Michael Brennan detailed with beautiful resonance Siobhán's great spirit and her wonderful, loving character. He told the congregation that their presence was of huge importance to her parents Andi and Brid, and her sisters Áine and Fiona. While Fr Brennan celebrated the mass with five other priests from Connemara, the secondary school choir from Scoil Chuimsitheach Chiaráin sang to the accompaniment of harp and guitar.

Some students, overcome with grief, had to leave the

church. During the sermon, school friends presented gifts that reflected their memories of Siobhán. Her teddy clown symbolised her deep love for her family, while her school diary reflected her bond with her classmates as well as friendships formed during her time at school. A picture which she had painted was presented as a confirmation of her love of art. Another friend carried one of Siobhán's favourite CDs and presented it as a symbol of her passion for music.

At the end of the mass Siobhán's uncle Ciarán Ó Fatharta thanked the congregation for their support and commended the gardaí on their investigation efforts. He then made an emotional appeal for help to try to find Siobhán's killer. On concluding his speech he asked the congregation to show a sign of appreciation for 'Siobhán's seventeen lovely years'. The mourners responded with rapturous applause.

Afterwards, as the coffin was removed from the church, a guard of honour was formed by Siobhán's classmates.

Garda investigators were among the mourners, a part of the upsurge of grief, but their thoughts were also firmly focused on tracking down the man responsible for this atrocity. They knew already from the geography of where the body was found that the perpetrator had to have local knowledge that no passing stranger could possess. Only a person with thorough knowledge of the area could have found Tismeán beach that night. While a dark cloud hung over the area, for many months the team gathered evidence that would stand up in court, concentrating on a prime suspect – John 'Demesne' McDonagh.

After being seen in the vicinity of the car where Siobhán was, he disappeared from the witness radar between 11.50 p.m. and 2.10 a.m. when he arrived in An Feadóg chip shop where he started a row with another man. But in advance of that witnesses had seen him driving his distinctive Ford Mondeo car from the direction of Tismeán beach.

When questioned – without that knowledge – he claimed to have spent all of the night in Carraroe. But there was a gap of two hours and twenty minutes that he could not account for and was not supported by other witness evidence. When he was asked to produce the clothes he was wearing on the night he gave detectives different clothes to those recorded on CCTV.

Investigators knew immediately that he was lying. They secured a warrant to search his house and his car. The clothes he had worn on the night of the murder were seized and his car was impounded for forensic examination.

Forensic expert Dr Louise McKenna's examination of both the clothes and the car yielded fibre evidence that proved that McDonagh had been in contact with Siobhán Hynes on the night, a direct contradiction of his statement to detectives that he had no contact with Siobhán on the night. Numerous fibres on the suspect's white T-shirt matched those from Siobhán's blue polyester fleece jacket and wine acrylic jumper.

Fibres from the victim's socks were found on the front and back of his white T-shirt. Fibres from her fleece were found on the passenger seat of the Mondeo while fibres from the red fluffy car seat cover matched two red fibres found on Siobhán's clothes. When confronted with these implicating facts McDonagh still denied any involvement in the murder.

Investigators deduced that it would not have been hard for McDonagh to lure Siobhán into the car under some pretext, perhaps of giving her a lift home. One way or another he got her into his Ford Mondeo and began the short 3 km journey toward Tismeán beach – a lonely and remote spot. McDonagh knew it like the back of his hand, as his house was within a few minutes walking distance of the location.

He stopped the car before a gate and quickly overpowered the young girl, grabbing her by the throat first and forcing her out of the car. He then tore at her body and pulled away her clothes and underwear, viciously raping her with an instrument that has never been found. He defiled other parts of her body as well. While it is not unknown for sexual psychopaths to inflict such injuries, particularly after death, it is likely that McDonagh could not perform direct sexual rape possibly because he was impotent from the amount of alcohol he had consumed. This would have increased his rage and fuelled his already deep-seated hatred of women. For him his victim had no identity and was just an object to use to vent his perverted and violent lust.

He then put back on some of Siobhán's clothes. After the ferocity of the attack it is likely that Siobhán was unconscious at this stage. He then lifted her prone, battered body over the gate and continued another 300 metres along a rocky pathway.

He placed her in a crevice, sure that the tide would wash her body out to sea, and threw some of her belongings into the waves trying to wipe out further trace of the victim's identity. What began as a random and unplanned attack now took on the mask of cold calculation as the killer tried to remove evidence he thought might tie him to the crime. All he cared for now was himself. He was going to make sure that, by leaving the injured teenager to her inevitable fate, she would never identify him as her attacker.

There was not an iota of mercy in the mind of John McDonagh. Without a trace of remorse he returned to his car, drove back to Carraroe to the chip shop and caused a row to give the impression he had never left the vicinity, a plan that he had clearly hatched on the drive back.

However, what he had in brawn he lacked in brains. Whatever commotion he could create to draw attention to himself could never explain the time he was missing from the town. On a Saturday night there were a lot more people about who might see him driving away or coming back or who would notice his absence.

Even more astounding and symptomatic of his poor intelligence was his lack of forensic awareness. He had left himself wide open by not getting rid of the most important evidence – the clothes he wore on the night and anything, however small, that might have been left behind in his car by the presence of the victim.

The hunt ground on until the investigation team assembled enough evidence that would ensure a strong case and a conviction. On the morning of June 18, 1999, McDonagh was woken from sleep in his lorry which was parked in a compound in Maynooth. He was arrested by Superintendent Jim Sugrue in the company of four other gardaí. He did not attempt to feign surprise and willingly extended his hands to be cuffed. With a casual half smile he quietly said, 'Put them on, I was expecting ye.' But it was in no way an admission of his part in the crime, it was just a typical smart man remark to give him some imagined dignity as he was being led away.

A month later he was given bail on an independent surety of £15,000 in the High Court on condition he kept out of the counties Galway, Mayo, Clare and Westmeath until the hearing of the case. For a man who had committed such a heinous crime and displayed such violent and perverted tendencies to women, this was another example of the ludicrous nature of our justice system. If anyone should have been kept on remand, it was McDonagh.

Due to a huge backlog of rape and murder cases, it took two years for the case to come to trial. During that time he proved his dangerous and violent inclinations. He was convicted of soliciting a prostitute in Clondalkin and allegedly raped another prostitute and attempted to strangle her. The victim was so terrified by her ordeal that she could not pick her attacker out at an identity parade.

The trial began in May 2001 and after a six-week hearing involving testimonies from 170 witnesses, the day of reckoning arrived on June 17 when the jury's verdict was greeted with shouts of approval from supporters of the victim.

McDonagh was found guilty of murder and rape, the former bringing a sentence of life and the latter, ten years to run concurrently.

McDonagh reacted emotionally to the result. He threw up his arms and, dropping to his knees, roared, 'For fuck's sake, ní dhearna mé é (I didn't do it).' He then burst into tears and sat sobbing. It was clear that right down to the wire the killer believed that he would walk free. While he lied about what happened on the night of December 5, 1998, the forensics told the truth.

But for the Hynes family the nightmare will never end.

11
DEATH OF A CHILD
BEAUTY QUEEN

Murder of any sort is the unacceptable face of violence in all society, but the deliberate, unlawful killing of a child holds a particular resonance because it spells the death of innocence and paints the worst nightmare of all parents in any part of the world. A child has no past to speak of and without that child there is no future for the parents, only an endless haunting of what might have been and will never be.

Imagine if that child was murdered in the family home and the parents became the prime suspects and, without the crime being solved, having to live forever with the shadow of suspicion hanging over them, that suspicion bolstered unrelentingly by the investigating authorities and the media.

This was the scenario in the case of six-year-old JonBenet Ramsey, described by the media as a painted baby, a sexualised toddler, a beauty queen. And found dead in the basement of the family home in Boulder, Colorado on December 26, 1996.

For some time prior to the murder of their daughter, John and Patsy Ramsey's life was the stuff of the American dream, ideal in every aspect with fortune smiling unequivocally in their favour. Patsy was a former beauty queen, John a highly successful businessman. They moved to Boulder in 1991 where John started a computer company in his garage.

Boulder, twenty-six miles northwest of Denver, is an old-fashioned small town with many houses dating from the thirties. Its population of 100,000 has roughly one third affiliated with the University of Colorado. It has nice, well laid out neighbourhoods and, by all accounts, a very good quality of life far from the madding crowds of the big cities.

Beautiful mountains in the background, a lot of people into jogging and the healthy life of mountain walks and trekking, it was an ideal place to live the good life and bring up kids in a rarefied environment. It had lots of facilities, a hundred restaurants and little crime of any substantial dimension.

The values, it might be said, were old-fashioned and the instincts, born of a professional ethos, liberal. However the killing of a six-year-old child challenged these values in a manner that the inhabitants and the authorities could never imagine.

From modest beginnings John Ramsey's business thrived and he and Patsy built a large house in an upmarket suburb. Life was not just good, it was beyond their wildest dreams. They became popular and desirable neighbours and entertained regularly and lavishly.

In May 1996, John's business Access Graphics had been bought over by Lockheed-Martin while he still continued to run the firm. He had a net personal worth of over six million dollars.

The Ramseys' home was what some people might describe as an ostentatious reflection of this wealth, which was more down to Patsy who had been in charge of the renovations and decoration after they moved in. John Ramsey, despite his success, was a man of reserved character; if you did not know he was a wealthy man, he would never give that impression.

With a redbrick Tudor façade, the house measured 6,866 square feet of living space and occupied almost half an acre. Inside, rooms were decorated with flowered carpets and vivid colours. The livingroom was reproduction French décor and expensive oil paintings hung on the walls.

The kitchen was large but practical and behind it, just inside a patio door, was a spiral staircase which led to the second floor. From the second floor landing there was direct access to two bedrooms and a playroom. There were two further bedrooms on this floor. JonBenet's bedroom on the second floor was closest to the spiral staircase. A staircase led to the third-floor master bedroom.

JonBenet's room was full of shelves containing cartoon and Shirley Temple videos and her wardrobe was chock-a-block with clothes. Her pageant costumes were in her half-sister Melinda's bedroom, and were evidence of her mother's obsession with her daughter as a pageant queen.

JonBenet's half-brother John's bedroom was next door to hers and her brother Burke's room was on the same level but separated by the playroom. Melinda and John, both in their twenties, lived away from home.

On the third floor John and Patsy Ramsey's bedroom was

very large with a view of the mountains. No less than twenty-three of their daughter's pageant trophies were on shelves and on the floor.

The cluttered basement had a number of rooms connected by a hallway. One contained a train set. Down a short hall was the boiler room. At the rear of this a door led to the wine cellar.

It is clear that the Ramseys' opulent living quarters provided a virtual maze that anyone would have great difficulty negotiating unless they were familiar with it.

The last party the Ramseys hosted was just three days before Christmas 1996, with a hundred guests. They had every reason to celebrate: Patsy had beaten ovarian cancer and John had been voted Boulder's businessman of the year. Apparently, adversity had been left behind. This Christmas had 'special' written all over it for the Ramseys. Heaven, however, was soon going to transform into hell.

On Christmas night they attended a party in the neighbourhood at the home of their best friends, the White family, just a few blocks away. On the way back JonBenet had fallen asleep in the car, so they carried her upstairs to her room and put her to bed at round 9.30 p.m. Shortly afterwards they retired, as they planned to get up early for a trip to their holiday home on Lake Michigan. Eleven-year-old Burke was asleep in his own room.

The following morning Patsy woke up after 5 a.m. and went downstairs to the kitchen. At the foot of the stairs she found a ransom note, unusually long at two and a half pages.

Addressed to Mr Ramsey, it claimed that JonBenet had been kidnapped by a local faction who threatened to kill her if certain instructions were not followed.

> *Mr. Ramsey.*
>
> *Listen carefully! We are a group of individuals that represent a small foreign faction. We ~~xx~~ respect your bussiness but not the country that it serves. At this time we have your daughter in our posession. She is safe and unharmed and if you want her to see 1997, you must follow our instructions to the letter.*
>
> *You will withdraw $118,000.00 from your account. $100,000 will be in $100 bills and the remaining $18,000 in $20 bills. Make sure that you bring an adequate size attache to the bank. When you get home you will put the money in a brown paper bag. I will call you between 8 and 10 am tomorrow to instruct you on delivery. The delivery will be exhausting so I advise you to be rested. If we monitor you getting the money early, we might call you early to arrange an earlier delivery of the money and hence a earlier ~~delivery~~ pickup of your daughter.*
>
> *Any deviation of my instructions will result in the immediate execution of your daughter. You will also be denied her remains for proper burial. The two gentlemen watching over your daughter do not particularly like you so I advise you not to provoke them. Speaking to anyone about your situation, such as Police, F.B.I., etc., will result in your daughter being beheaded. If we catch you talking to*

a stray dog, she dies. If you alert bank authorities, she dies. If the money is in any way marked or tampered with, she dies. You will be scanned for electronic devices and if any are found, she dies. You can try to deceive us but be warned that we are familiar with Law enforcement countermeasures and tactics. You stand a 99% chance of killing your daughter if you try to out smart us. Follow our instructions and you stand a 100% chance of getting her back. You and your family are under constant scrutiny as well as the authorities. Don't try to grow a brain John. You are not the only fat cat around so don't think that killing will be difficult. Don't underestimate us John. Use that good southern common sense of yours.

It is up to you now John!
Victory!
S.B.T.C

Patsy yelled to John as she ran up the stairs and opened the door to JonBenet's room. Finding it empty, they made the decision to phone the police. Patsy rang after 5.45 a.m. Within seven minutes police officers Karl Veitch and Rick French arrived at the fifteen-room Ramsey mansion.

A cursory search of the house including the basement was made. By the time Detective Linda Arndt arrived at 8 a.m. with Det Fred Patterson, friends of the Ramseys, Fleet and Priscilla White, John Fernie and his wife Barbara and local minister Rev Rol Hoverstock, were all at the residence as well as a crime scene investigator and a victim counsellor.

Patsy Ramsey told Det Arndt she had gone downstairs shortly after 5 a.m. to make coffee. She had descended the back spiral stairway as she normally did and at the bottom of the steps she had found the three pages of paper laid across a stair step.

John Ramsey called a bank to make arrangements to have the ransom money available.

Det Arndt attached a tape recorder to the phone and asked that John Ramsey be the only one to answer it. She instructed him to tell the kidnappers that he could not get hold of the money until 5 p.m. and to ask to speak to his daughter, to establish that she was alive. Det Arndt asked him if he could think of anyone who would want to hurt him by this course of action.

As 10 a.m. passed John Ramsey seemed to get more nervous while his wife just kept repeating the phrase, 'Why did they do this?' But as the morning wore slowly on, investigators were questioning the veracity of the ransom note and its most unusual form.

Eventually the thin investigation team, depleted by leave, began to secure the crime scene, first ordering the sealing of JonBenet's bedroom and limiting any non-essential personnel to one area.

It was established that there were no signs of a break-in. There were no footprints on the light dusting of snow that surrounded the house. However, this was misleading as there was no snow around most of the perimeter of the house. A

Boulder County police officer at the scene noticed that his steps left no visible footprints.

At 1 p.m. when no call had come from the kidnappers, Det Arndt asked John Ramsey, Fleet White and John Fernie to go through the house to check for any sign of JonBenet or anything that might have been left or taken that belonged to her. This was a major blunder by an officer not sufficiently familiar with the protocol at a crime scene. The search should have been conducted by crime scene officers and not members of the family or friends who would inevitably contaminate vital evidence.

Fernie stayed on the ground floor while John Ramsey and Fleet White searched the basement. In the room where Burke had his train set there was a broken window which Ramsey explained by telling his friend he had broken it some months before when he found himself locked out. The window was closed but unlatched.

They moved to the boiler room and through this to the wine cellar. Ramsey pulled the door open, and peered into the darkness. He then reached for a switch inside and turned on the light. There was a white blanket in the middle of the floor with two small hands sticking out from under the blanket.

Fleet White heard his friend cry out, 'Oh my God, oh my God.' From a distance of twelve feet he saw his friend enter the room and turn left out of sight. He followed him in and saw him leaning down towards the blanket.

A police report describes what happened.

John Ramsey went to the basement of the

house, followed by Fleet White. Within a few minutes, Fleet came running up the stairs, grabbed the telephone in the back office located on the first floor and yelled for someone to call for an ambulance.

Detective Arndt ran to the front of the house, where the door leading to the basement was located. Det Arndt saw John Ramsey was carrying a young girl in his arms. Both arms of the girl were raised above her head. There appeared to be a string hanging from the girl's right wrist. The girl's lips were blue; she appeared to have livor mortis [internal blood pooling] on the back side of her body; she had rigor mortis; she was not breathing. JonBenet was dressed in a light-coloured long-sleeved turtleneck and light-coloured pants (similar to pyjama bottoms). John Ramsey placed the girl onto the floor, inside the front door. The girl was identified by John Ramsey as being JonBenet. JonBenet was not breathing; her body was cool to the touch; she had a white cloth strung around her neck similar to the cloth string around the wrist; there was a red circular mark at the front of her neck about the size of a quarter at the base of her throat; she had an odour of decay to her, she had dried mucus from one of her nostrils.

Based on Det Arndt's experience, JonBenet appeared to have been dead for a period of time.

John Ramsey told the detective that he had found JonBenet in the wine cellar in the basement, underneath a blanket with her wrists tied above her head and a piece of tape covering her mouth. John Ramsey had removed the tape from her mouth before he carried her upstairs.

Det Arndt asked Fleet White to guard the door to the basement and not allow anyone in. She asked Ramsey to tell his wife and then covered the wound on JonBenet's neck with the child's long-sleeved shirt. When Ramsey returned he put a blanket over JonBenet and lay down beside her and hugged her. Even allowing for the grief of a father, the crime scene officer should never have allowed that action. It demonstrated that the Boulder force had little or no experience in the preservation of serious crime scenes. Patsy Ramsey was led into the room by Fernie's wife, and she also hugged her dead daughter in a display of understandable grief, one which she and her husband should have been prevented from doing by Det Arndt. There was already more than enough contamination of the crime scene. The whole house should have been immediately sealed off and family and neighbours confined to one small area. Once it was sealed a comprehensive and thorough search should have been carried out by law enforcement officers. John Ramsey and his friends should never have been allowed to search the house.

Fifteen minutes later in answer to Det Arndt's page, FBI

agent Ron Walker and Boulder Detective Sgt Larry Mason arrived at the house. They went downstairs to the wine cellar where they noted the white blanket and the piece of duct tape discarded by John Ramsey. There was also a pink Barbie nightgown. The detectives thought there was something strange about the scene but they could not then pinpoint it. Mason went about securing the house, clearing it of everyone except investigators.

It would have been entirely in keeping with best practice for Boulder police commander John Eller to call in the FBI kidnap experts from the child abduction unit to help with the investigation. FBI procedure would be to investigate the parents first, then extended family, friends, work colleagues and when this process was completed to turn their attention to the possibility of strangers. The statistics supported this approach – the vast majority of victims found in the family home have been murdered by relatives.

The fact was that the Boulder Police Department had neither the resources nor the experience to deal with this case which, if not handled properly, would become impossibly complex and much more difficult to solve. But Commander Eller, an old-style cop wary of the whole culture of the FBI and Quantico, was determined that his men could do the job.

While the Ramseys went to stay with friends, the house became a crime scene. However it was too late as already that crime scene had been trampled over and vital evidence seriously compromised. The investigation team began to focus on family members. The finger of suspicion was on John

Ramsey and a search warrant affidavit was filed the very same day that the body was removed. Police wanted to search for fibres, notepads, felt-tipped pens and any other evidence. But already Eller's team were losing time on every front. It took them six hours to put together the application for the search warrant. Eller would have learnt in police academy that in the situation that he was now facing, a murder as opposed to a kidnap, the first twenty-four hours is vital. This delay also held up the medical examiner who would carry out the preliminary on-scene examination of the body before the full autopsy.

By 8 p.m. the search warrant had been obtained and the house could be searched from top to bottom. The ransom notes and writing pads obtained from the house were sent to the Colorado Bureau of Investigation where the state's scientific lab was located. Shortly afterwards the medical examiner Dr John Meyer arrived to examine the body which was lying under the lighted Christmas tree. A preliminary examination took place and later the body of JonBenet was removed to the Boulder Community Hospital in preparation for the full postmortem the following morning, December 27.

For operational reasons, the full details of the postmortem findings would not be released into the public domain for a long time. But in the interim there would be sufficient leaks to keep the media and public appetite for the case satisfied.

As the postmortem was being carried out, newsroom staff in the local paper *The Daily Camera* were reacting to what they perceived to be the biggest story of the year. With a dearth of information, the front page lead was straightforward.

MISSING GIRL FOUND DEAD

A six-year-old Boulder girl, reported kidnapped early Thursday, was found dead in her parents' home later that afternoon. It is Boulder's first official homicide of 1996. Boulder police said a family member discovered the body of JonBenet Ramsey in the basement of the family house at about 1.30 p.m.

Police detectives and crime scene investigators began searching the house late Thursday after securing a search warrant. No details of what they found were disclosed.

Although the official cause of death was not yet known, Police Chief Tom Korby said the case is considered a homicide. The child had not been shot or stabbed, said Detective Sgt Larry Mason. No arrest had been made as of press time, and police had no suspects, Mason said.

The Boulder County coroner's office refused to discuss details of the case, though an autopsy will be performed today, according to city spokeswoman Leslie Aaholm.

The child was the 1995 Little Miss Colorado and a student at Martin Park Elementary School, according to a family friend. Patsy

Ramsey travelled around the country with JonBenet to attend her beauty contests. 'They were so serious about this beauty-queen stuff, but they never put any pressure on her,' said Dee Dee Nelson-Schneider, a family friend. 'She had her own float in the Colorado Parade of Lights in December 1995, and Patsy walked along the side of the float the whole parade to make sure JonBenet was safe. That's how protective Patsy was.'

Elliot Zaret and Alli Krupski
Daily Camera, December 27, 1996.

Further investigation established a white cord was wrapped tightly around JonBenet's neck. The same cord was tied loosely to her wrists. The broken handle of a paintbrush measuring approximately 11 cm in length, had been tied to the cord to form a garrotte. There was a thin gold ring on the middle finger of her right hand, and a bracelet with her name engraved on one side and a date 12.25.96 on the other. A red heart was drawn on the palm of her left hand. Around her neck was a gold chain with a single cross attached. Evidence suggested that someone took her, by force or otherwise, from her bedroom to the kitchen where she had eaten some pineapple, undigested pieces of which were found in her stomach at the postmortem. She was then taken to the basement, had tape placed over her mouth and was bound with the nylon cord. She was sexually interfered with and strangled with the garrotte. There were also injuries to her head.

According to the police report, JonBenet was last seen alive at approximately 10 p.m. on December 25. When police first saw the body at 1.05 p.m. on December 26, it was completely set with rigor mortis which indicates that she had died between 10 p.m. on the previous evening and 6 a.m. on December 26. Police also reported the smell of decomposition. The rate of decomposition depends on a number of factors but for the odour of decomposition to have been detected, JonBenet would have to have died near the beginning of the time frame.

There were a number of matters arising from the aftermath of the killing. Firstly, there was no obvious evidence that pointed to a break-in or forced entry. Secondly, it would have been entirely natural for the parents to search the house, even after discovering the ransom note, as it could have been fake. Thirdly, when Patsy Ramsey called the police, she never mentioned the threat in the note that if she followed that course of action her daughter would be 'beheaded'. The Ramseys also brought neighbours to the house, ignoring the other threat in the note that if they were caught talking to a stray dog JonBenet would die. If the note was genuine and it included the warning that they were under constant scrutiny, this was not only taking a huge risk but was tantamount to signing their daughter's death warrant.

Fourthly, when sent on the search by the detective, John Ramsey found the body very quickly. John Ramsey was an intelligent man, a hugely successful businessman. He must have known that after finding his daughter's body, the last thing to do was touch it, not to mind move it from the site where it was found. JonBenet had been dead for quite a while. Even in a state of shock this was an odd and might seem a somewhat deliberate action.

Fifthly, a writing pad was found in the house which was the source of the ransom note. What kidnapper would wait to get to the house of the intended victim to search for a piece of paper to write the note and take the extra risk of being caught?

Finally, the total sum of the ransom money demanded was exactly the amount that John Ramsey had received as a bonus, and tiny by comparison to his multi-millionaire status and the billion dollar status of his company. If there was a kidnap gang, its members were rank amateurs. It was yet another odd fact needing explanation which made the investigators focus more on the Ramsey household rather than on an outside agency or persons.

On the other hand, what possible motive could there be for the Ramseys to murder their lovely young daughter? The only possibility might be to cover up an initial attack or beating of her that went wrong.

There were many questions to be answered but the finger of suspicion was pointing in one direction only – John and Patsy Ramsey. Justified or not, there was no balance in the manner in which the media and police sources combined to begin what quickly became a witch hunt. On the other hand, the Ramseys with what seemed indecent haste began to hire lawyers, ostensibly to protect themselves. From what, the police and the public might justifiably ask, if they were innocent as they maintained they were?

On December 29, four days after the murder, a memorial service for JonBenet was held at a local church. The mourning was not going to divert the attention of the media. An article in *Vanity Fair* suggested that John Ramsey had left the house before the police arrived using an excuse that he was going to get the mail. The story was false but the police did not deny it or make any attempt to correct it.

By Monday, December 30, the Ramseys had returned to Atlanta, where they were originally from and where JonBenet was born, to bury their daughter. Again, a story was run about how they got there, that John flew the family in his private jet. This was also false. The jet belonged to Lockheed-Martin, the company that had purchased Access Graphics, and was flown by a company pilot.

JonBenet's funeral took place on New Year's Eve 1996 at her parents' family church in Atlanta. Even as they buried their daughter a new media story emerged that they had hired several criminal lawyers. Although their friend, a lawyer, Mike Bynum had hired the attorneys, it was perceived as another indication of the parents' guilt. Alarmed at the mounting criticism, Bynum and members of the family urged the Ramseys to go on television and defend themselves. The following day they appeared on CNN.

At this stage in time, they had not been interviewed by

investigators which, by any proper due process, they should have been. But that was down to the Boulder Police Department and the District Attorney's office, both of whose reluctance on the matter was mystifying. Sensitivity is only one tiny part of a murder investigation.

One of the questions during the interview was: 'Do you believe that someone outside your home killed JonBenet?' Tearfully, Patsy answered:

> There is a killer on the loose, I don't know who it is, I don't know if it's a he or a she but if I were a resident of Boulder, I would tell my friends to keep their babies close.

The interview was not a PR triumph because it gave the impression that the Ramseys were putting up a front and would rather talk on television than talk to the investigation team.

The next day the mayor of Boulder, Leslie Durgan, gave a press conference to refute Patsy's statement, claiming:

> People in Boulder have no need to fear that there is someone wandering the streets, as has been portrayed by some people, looking for young people to attack. Boulder is safe, it's always been a safe community and it continues to be a safe community.

This was an extraordinary statement a week after the brutal slaying of a six-year-old child; it was patently obvious that an event of this magnitude did not copper-fasten the safety record of the town.

But the questions were asked in a public arena, not in the privacy of a police interrogation room. The death of the young pageant queen was descending into farce.

The Ramseys were understandably outraged by the implications of the mayor's statement but were also realising this was what the majority of people were thinking. Their strategy of surrounding themselves with lawyers and a public relations consultant was fuelling the reaction.

Divisions within the Boulder Police Department and resistance to the D.A.'s office which would be revealed later, were creating even worse problems for the investigation. The separate lines of action would provide easy meat for the gathering hungry hordes of the media.

The Ramsey family had hardly returned to Boulder than news stories began to appear reporting that police believed the murdered girl had been sexually assaulted prior to her killing. Television footage of JonBenet's beauty pageants, displaying a young girl made up and dressed, in some instances, in provocative costumes, with the undertone that the Ramseys might have sexually abused her brought a hunting pack of 300 journalists to Boulder.

Half a century on from the Black Dahlia this murder had also become the subject of a ratings war in the media. In the rush, inaccurate and false stories spread and were repeated in epidemic proportions. The thrust of the criticism of the Ramseys was for degrading their daughter in sexualised pageants and for hiring two lawyers. Also, they were accused of not cooperating with the police and delaying the investigation.

Brian Morgan, their attorney, vigorously denied the last charge pointing out that his clients had been interviewed on December 26 and 27. They had given samples of blood, hair and fingerprints. They had also given five handwriting samples, voluntarily. 'To say that the Ramseys had not cooperated in the investigation is a gross mis-characterisation,' said Morgan.

They were dealt another blow when their adviser, Bynum, told them that, unknown to them, the police had at first refused to release the body of their girl until they agreed to be interrogated. Even though Bynum had been successful in getting the body released, the police were now pressing for more interviews. The Ramseys took the view that, 'The police weren't there to help us, they were there to hang us.' Given the merciless nature of the press coverage and the constant leaking of bits from the investigation team, it would be hard not to feel sympathetic towards the Ramseys.

The bare fact of the matter was that the Ramseys had still not been interviewed formally by investigators, and if they had by this stage, they would not have been put on trial by the media with the same justification. This was a big mistake on their part, probably more so on the part of their legal advisers, and it was going to do them more harm than good, as it quickly emerged.

Another leak from police records indicated that warrants

had been sought to search the house for pornographic material. The media had a field day and carried stories of how the father's deviant sexual behaviour had resulted in the death of his daughter.

There were further unfounded allegations that John Ramsey had frequented a pornographic bookstore in downtown Denver. No proof was offered to back this story up. One story revealed that JonBenet had been taken to a local paediatric clinic twenty-seven times over a four-year period, the inference being that she had been sexually abused. The paediatrician said that he never found any evidence of this.

Ramsey's family, including his son John and daughter Melinda from his previous marriage and his ex-wife, told interviewers that he had always been a loving and gentle person who cherished his children and never abused them in any way.

Every allegation that had been made eventually was proven to be without substance but any lack of hard evidence against the Ramseys did not inhibit the media.

The host of an American talk show conducted a live 'murder trial' with a judge and a jury. The verdict was that John and Patsy Ramsey were considered liable for the wrongful death of their daughter JonBenet. The Ramseys, the ultimate Americans until now, were discovering that this could only happen in America.

The programme *Hard Copy* later ran a story by *Globe* magazine which alleged that JonBenet had gone to her parents' bedroom on the night of the murder because she had wet her own bed. The programme suggested, 'The most likely scenario is that her frazzled mum completely lost it and battered her.'

A terrible tragedy had degenerated into a public spectacle. Truth was going to be the loser.

The editor of Boulder newspaper *The Daily Camera*, Barrie Hartman, summed up the coverage:

> One of the failings that we in the news media
> have is that when we have stories that the
> tabloids have reported, we feel obliged to report
> on them as well, which can cause us some
> problems. I think JonBenet was a good example
> of that, where the details are repeated before
> they are verified as facts.

In May 1997 the Ramseys gave a press conference and John Ramsey at one point stared directly at the camera and stated emphatically: 'I did not kill my daughter JonBenet.' He later told an interviewer in relation to trial by media:

> Where is our common sense as a race of people?
> We've got a cancer in American society, in the
> form of our system of information. We're going
> to take a shot at trying to fix it and that's what we
> are trying to do here.

Despite John Ramsey's protestation he would learn that the media do not go away. To defend himself and his wife he engaged the media on an ongoing basis, giving the impression – do they protest too much? It was a choice the Ramseys made instead of maintaining a dignified silence in the face of undignified coverage.

The years passed and yet there seemed to be no let up, the case of the killing of the young pageant beauty queen would not go away. There would be books, more books, documentaries, a TV mini-series and more developments, what a Shakespearean tragedy might term 'sound and fury'. The JonBenet murder had all the elements of one of the Bard's tragic epics.

Almost three years on, members of the District Attorney Alex Hunter's prosecution team met with Dr Henry Lee, the famous criminalist, to discuss the forensic testing that had been conducted during the case. The tests that had been processed by the Colorado Bureau of Investigation were based on samples that had been taken from the victim's fingernail scrapings, blood from her panties and hair samples.

Some of these were said to have contained traces of the victim's blood and other DNA evidence. So far, tests on the Ramsey family and other suspects failed to provide any matches. Such a long time had elapsed it was little wonder that no other physical evidence emerged.

Three days after the meeting D.A. Hunter called a press conference to announce that a grand jury had been assembled thirteen months earlier to hear evidence in the case. A grand jury hearing is not a court case where cross-examination takes place. The deliberations result only in a recommendation but it would be a testing ground if a case ever came to court. The grand jury found that there was insufficient evidence to charge anyone with the murder of JonBenet. It seemed that should have been the end of that. The prosecution could come up with nothing and now an independent body had come to the same conclusion.

Three weeks afterwards, however, Bill Owens, the Governor of Colorado, told interviewers that he still considered John Ramsey a prime suspect in the murder. Owens made the statement after John Ramsey had offered to meet him in an attempt to convince the governor to appoint a special prosecutor to oversee the case. The response was:

Mr Ramsey is considered to be a prime suspect,

it would be very inappropriate to meet him.

The governor wasn't the only one to point the finger of blame. Newly appointed Boulder police chief Mark Beckner, regardless of the failure of the grand jury to indict anybody, stated that as far as he was concerned the Ramseys were 'still under an umbrella of suspicion'.

By the end of October 1999 the Ramseys threatened legal action over what they termed 'slanderous remarks'. In response, Troy Eid, chief legal officer for the governor, said that he believed that Governor Owens was within his rights when he suggested that the Ramseys quit hiding behind their attorneys and cooperate with investigators looking for their daughter's killer, no matter where that trail may lead.

In any event the lawyer said that the governor was well

within his constitutional rights to say what he did, being protected by the First Amendment in his role as a public official.

Continuing to be the target of politicians and the media, and with no meaningful recourse, the Ramseys decided to tell the story from their perspective and signed an exclusive book deal with a Nashville-based publisher which specialised in religious books. The Ramseys said their book, entitled *The Death of Innocence,* would make the world aware of their innocence and their faith in God. John Ramsey came out fighting at a press conference stating,

> We have patiently waited for the justice process to evolve in the matter of our daughter's death. We have remained silent while baseless and slanderous accusations about our family were made by the frenzied media. The time is appropriate to recount our experiences in this tragedy.

At the same time, in a move that would further alienate the media, they appointed a prominent Atlanta libel lawyer, L. Lin Wood, hired on a contingency basis, earning a percentage of any damages won. In their book the Ramseys gave their view of who might have been responsible which included: one of the Ramseys' former housekeepers who may have intended to kidnap JonBenet because she was having money troubles; a man who played Santa Claus at the Ramseys' Christmas party the week she was killed; a former Access Graphics' employee who was extremely agitated with John Ramsey after he left; a local man and former freelance writer whose girlfriend reported that he was acting suspiciously the day after the murder and seemed overly agitated by the killing.

The Boulder Police Department chief Mark Beckner told reporters that all the people suggested as suspects in the book had been individually investigated and were no longer considered as active suspects.

The Ramseys offered the theory that the crime was a kidnapping which went wrong. The attacker's plan could have failed when JonBenet woke up and recognised her assailant, turning the would-be kidnapper into a killer.

The Ramseys criticised the Boulder police department and of course targeted the media, likening them to 'vultures waiting to find tidbits of flesh to pounce on.' They explained how they cooperated with police on sixteen different occasions.

The City of Boulder and the State of Colorado had spent a combined total of over $2 million on the investigation. Hunter's annual budget was approved in November, none of which was allocated to the JonBenet Ramsey murder case. D.A. Alex Hunter said that he had no immediate plans to seek more funding to keep the investigation going. Police and prosecution files were put into storage as the case began to be wound down although the file would be left open to facilitate the handling of any new development of evidence.

Who did it? Two theories

At the end of 1998 there was another twist to the saga when Lou Smit, a former member of the prosecution team, announced that he was working with John and Patsy Ramsey to prove the theory that an intruder killed the child. Smit, then aged sixty-three, a former El Paso murder investigator and a veteran of more than 150 Colorado murder cases, had previously come out of retirement in March 1997 to work with D.A. Alex Hunter on the investigation. He resigned on September 20, 1998, because he was concerned that the investigation was, in his opinion, wrongly targeting the Ramseys. He claimed there was ample evidence that an intruder was responsible.

Just over one month earlier another senior member of the investigation team, Steve Thomas, would also resign but for different reasons. The detective resigned from the Boulder police force after he discovered that the district attorney's office had advised detectives on the JonBenet case that they would not be participating as grand jury advisory witnesses.

Thomas's letter of resignation revealed deep divisions between the Boulder Police Department and the county prosecutor's office. This division and the perceived reluctance of the Ramseys to cooperate, Thomas believed, was shielding the murderer.

His resignation letter to Chief Beckner dated August 6, 1998, told a lot about police frustration with the investigation, concluding that no one, particularly the D.A.'s office, wanted this murder to be solved. It showed that, apart from the bizarre aspects of this case, there was a fatal split at the heart of the prosecution effort. Justice it seemed was not the top priority. It also gave a depressing insight into the inefficient and over-cautious approach taken to the case by the district attorney's office.

Thomas claimed that the investigation was constantly subverted by the D.A.'s office. After thirteen years as an exemplary and decorated officer, he did not want to challenge the system but what he witnessed over his two-year involvement reduced him to tears. He wrote that at thirty-six years of age he was totally committed but he had to walk away from this 'travesty'.

Thomas's reasons for resigning provided a damning indictment of the role played by District Attorney Alex Hunter's office in the investigation. Interestingly enough there is not one mention of JonBenet's parents. An ominous sign, the reason for which would soon be revealed. Whatever the rights and wrongs of the case, or the validity of certain lines of investigation and value of evidence, there could be little chance of a successful outcome if the two most powerful institutions of prosecution were so radically divided.

It paints a depressing picture of the morale within the Boulder Police Department investigation team.

Thomas would later publish a book, *JonBenet: Inside the Ramsey Murder Investigation from a Leading Detective on the Case*, presenting a case the very opposite of his colleague Smit, alleging that Patsy Ramsey had killed her daughter accidentally and then attempted to cover it up with the collusion of her husband.

Did the parents of the dead beauty pageant queen have a case to answer? If JonBenet was not murdered by one or both of her parents or by her eleven-year-old brother Burke, the only people in the house that night, then she must have been killed by an intruder. Smit said intruder. Thomas said the Ramseys.

The basic method of murder investigation is in the earliest stage to draw up a list of possible suspects and concentrate on eliminating them, either by comparison with physical evidence or by checking their whereabouts at the time of the offence. Using this course of action the investigation team does not become side-tracked by suspects who seem suitable at the time. By using this process of elimination the list of suspects is narrowed considerably.

In the JonBenet case, even those just associated with the family amounted to a large number and would have taken a large task force considerable time to process. Other targets would have included someone with a history of child sex offences who may have frequented the pageant circuit or someone in the Boulder area who might have been involved in a child pornography ring. Such suspects have a motive but would also have to have been able to exploit the opportunity on the night of December 25 or the very early morning of December 26.

The opposing theory is that someone inside the house killed the victim and while the opportunity would have been much more straightforward, the motive would be much harder to prove.

A variety of news media speculated that the Ramseys were the principal suspects in the case, citing a number of clues that they focused upon. There was the supposed lack of footprints outside the house and no visible signs of forced entry. Police noted that the broken but tightly closed basement window had not been opened recently, because spider webs were still attached to its base when police checked on the day JonBenet's body was found.

Video footage shot on December 26, however, showed that large areas around the house had no snow cover. That should have dispensed with the no footprint theory as ruling out an intruder. Supporters of the intruder theory cite the basement window as an easy way to enter the house and move about undetected and unheard. They say that JonBenet's bedroom was one floor below her parents' bedroom, a total of fifty-five feet of floor covered by thick carpeting, making it ideal for a soundless approach. A carpeted spiral staircase, a few feet from the victim's room, led to the kitchen. From the kitchen it was only a few steps to the door that led to the basement stairs. At the bottom of the stairs, a short corridor led directly to the room where her body was found.

However to negotiate this the killer had to be someone familiar with the layout of the house. They would have to have known the Ramseys well enough to know that John Ramsey had received a bonus of $118,000, and had to be small enough to have gained entry via a narrow basement window and possibly exited the same way.

They would have to have been confident enough to spend the time, not only to commit the offence but also to have the presence of mind to write a long note in an attempt to draw suspicion away from themselves.

They would also have to have known JonBenet well enough to take her out of bed, into the kitchen and then to the basement.

The medical examiner Dr John Meyer's report on the body of JonBenet was thorough and extensive and as a scientific document made no interpretation of the physical facts. JonBenet died of ligature strangulation with a furrow caused by the cord around her neck, and an eight-inch long skull fracture with a piece of skull nearly an inch square broken loose. There was no laceration of the scalp as would be expected if she was struck by a flashlight or club. Experts said that this wound was more consistent with the head being bashed against a toilet or bathtub. The strangulation was effected by the killer using the broken handle of one of the parents' paintbrushes to tighten the cord around JonBenet's throat to choke her to death. There were abrasions on her back and legs that suggested to investigators that the body had been dragged to where it was found.

There were indications of sexual assault or what some experts would term as chronic sexual abuse. The second interpretation has been disputed. There was inflammation of the vaginal tract, a 1 cm by 1 cm opening in the hymen and traces of blood in the vaginal area and crotch of her panties. However this was carried out, it was not by penile penetration.

The sexual assault interpretation is not disputed but the abuse is contested by Denver medical examiner Dr Thomas Henry:

> From what is noted in the autopsy report, there is no evidence of injury to the anus, there is no evidence of injury to the skin around the vagina, the labia. There is no other indication from the autopsy report at all that there are any other previous injuries that have healed in that particular area.

In other words this opinion exonerates the Ramsey parents of any of the allegations that their daughter had been subjected to sexual abuse of any kind in advance of the murder. But, as in every aspect of this case, there are opposing and contradictory opinions.

Steve Thomas's book (written with Don Davis) when it was released in hardback in April 2000 and became a bestseller, left no doubt about whom he believed killed JonBenet. He writes that the murderer was JonBenet's panicked mother, Patsy Ramsey, and that her father John Ramsey opted to protect his wife in the investigation that followed.

Thomas theorised that an approaching fortieth birthday, the busy holiday season, an exhausting Christmas day and an argument with JonBenet had left her mother in a high state of emotion. After they came home from the Whites' party, JonBenet was hungry and her mother let her eat some pineapple. The kids were then put to bed.

Later, JonBenet woke up after wetting her bed and her annoyed mother wiped her quite harshly, which would explain the presence of dark fibres in her pubic region. This took place in the child's bathroom. The detective says that a row ensued and Patsy lost control, slamming her daughter's head against a hard surface with a force caused by rage but not originally intentional.

The child was now unconscious and the mother faced a dilemma: call for help, or find another explanation for JonBenet's impending death. There was no pressing need to make such a choice as, even if the doctors questioned the accident, little would have happened to Patsy in Boulder. But she panicked and moved the child down to the basement and hid her in the little room.

Thomas guessed that Patsy then went upstairs to the kitchen to write the ransom note. He claimed that the tear pattern of the ransom notepaper matched Patsy Ramsey's personal notepad, and the felt-tip pen used to write the note matched a pen found in a cup in the Ramseys' kitchen. She flipped to the middle of the writing tablet and started a ransom note, drafting one that ended on page 25. For some reason she discarded that one and ripped pages 15–25 from the tablet. Police never found those pages. On page 26 she began 'Mr and Mrs I' then abandoned the false start. At some point she drafted the long ransom note, creating the best piece of evidence.

She then faced the major problem of what to do with the body, deciding that leaving it in the distant almost inaccessible basement room was the best option. Thomas speculated that Patsy returned to the basement, a woman caught up in panic, where she could have seen – perhaps by detecting a faint heartbeat or a sound or a slight movement – that although completely unconscious JonBenet was not dead. She took the next step, looking for the closest available items in her desperation. Only feet away was her paint box. She grabbed a paintbrush and broke it to fashion a garrotte with some cord. She then looped the cord around her daughter's neck.

Then the staging continued to make it look more like a kidnapping. Patsy tied JonBenet's wrists, in front, not back, for otherwise the arms would not have been in the overhead position. But with a 35 cm length of cord between the wrists and the knot tied loosely over the clothing, there was no way this would have restrained a live child. It was a symbolic act to make it appear the child had been bound.

As part of her staging Thomas said that Patsy put a strip of duct tape over JonBenet's mouth.

For Thomas, Patsy not changing was the smoking gun. He knew that she was wearing the same clothes because a picture at the party on Christmas night showed her wearing a red turtleneck sweater and black pants. A Boulder police officer had noted in his report when he arrived at the Ramsey home on December 26 in response to the kidnapping emergency, Patsy was wearing a red turtleneck and black pants.

The woman, to whom looking good appeared always so important and who had a wardrobe full of designer clothes, had attended a party, come home late, put her children to bed, gone to sleep herself, arose early to fly across the country, put on fresh make-up and fixed her hair, and then put on the same clothes she had worn the previous night. 'Not likely, in my opinion,' Thomas wrote.

There was also the matter of the ransom note which the investigation team always considered their best piece of evidence. Thomas revealed that out of the seventy-three suspects whose writing samples were analysed by experts in comparison with the note, Patsy Ramsey was the only one who could not be excluded as its author.

He also accused her of changing her handwriting after the murder. Engaging the help of Don Foster, a Vassar college professor and one of the country's foremost linguistics experts, D.A. Alex Hunter had sent him a copy of the ransom note and writing samples from various suspects. After studying all the writing samples Foster told Det Thomas, 'I am going to conclude that the ransom note was the work of a single individual: Pat Ramsey.' He travelled to Boulder for a special briefing with investigators and representatives from the D.A.'s office and again confirmed his conclusion to them.

He dissected the ransom note and explained that the wording involved the intelligent and sometimes clever usage of language and said that the text suggested someone who was trying to deceive.

Foster, who had unmasked the Unabomber as well as the anonymous author of best seller *Primary Colours*, which satirised Bill Clinton's 1992 presidential campaign, was excluded from giving testimony to the grand jury. Foster would later change his mind about his assessment declaring that Patsy Ramsey was innocent.

Another point Thomas made about the note was that it was signed S.B.T.C. which stood for what the note described as a small foreign faction. Patsy had signed a Christmas note P.P.R.B.S.J. which she said stood for Patsy Paugh Ramsey, Bachelor of Science in Journalism, indicating her fondness of acronyms.

In mid March, 1997, retired detective Lou Smit outlined previously undisclosed evidence that led him to believe that the Ramseys were not responsible for their daughter's death.

> I believe that there's evidence of an intruder,
> and I believe people should be looking for him.
> There's a dangerous guy out there.

Smit was credited for having solved one of Colorado's most difficult crimes, the murder of thirteen-year-old Heather Dawn Church in her home in 1991. The teenager had vanished from her home one evening when her mother and two brothers had been at a scout meeting. Two years later her skeletal remains were found miles away in a ravine west of Colorado Springs.

Two years after this newly elected El Paso County Sheriff John Anderson asked Smit to take up the investigation into this cold case. He agreed and examined all the evidence, focusing his attention on a set of unidentified fingerprints found in the Church home and directed his detectives to send the prints to every state and law enforcement office in the country.

After contacting ninety-two different jurisdictions, a Louisiana police department matched the prints to Robert Charles Browne, a parolled thief who had moved to Colorado and was still living half a mile from the Church home three years after the killing. Browne later confessed to the murder saying that he had killed Heather with a blow to the head when she had discovered him robbing the home.

Sheriff Anderson had great respect for Smit's abilities, having trained under him in homicide investigation. 'He always had a sound method that started with the evidence and let it guide him towards the truth, rather than starting with a theory and forcing the evidence to fit it,' Anderson said.

According to Smit, there was plenty of evidence to support the intruder theory. Fibres on a metal baseball bat found outside the Ramseys' Boulder home matched a carpet found in the basement near the storage room where JonBenet's body was found. The bat was found 'in a place where kids normally wouldn't play,' Smit said, declining to elaborate.

DNA evidence, which indicated JonBenet's attacker was male but which did not match John Ramsey, was found on her body and panties.

Peanut-shaped foam packing material and leaves were found in the basement. Smit thinks these might have been brought inside by someone entering through the broken basement window. 'It would have been something that would not have been blown in there,' Smit said.

A suitcase below the broken window, which was moved there by someone other than the Ramseys, appeared to be the way the intruder boosted himself to exit the house.

Other evidence included a footprint found in the concrete dust of the wine cellar by a 'Hi-Tec' stamped hiking boot. The boot had not been connected to any of the Ramseys or the 400 people or more who had been to the house over the years.

An unidentified palm print was found on the door of the wine cellar. It did not belong to John, Patsy or Burke Ramsey.

A pubic hair was found on the blanket that JonBenet was wrapped in. It did not belong to John, Patsy or Burke Ramsey.

A piece of broken glass was found under the basement window.

Smit also theorised that JonBenet was subdued by the use of a stun gun and this was partially supported by Araphoe County Coroner Dr Michael Doberson: 'It looked to me, superficially, that it fits. There were marks on the victim's chin in portmortem photographs that could have been made by the electrodes of a stun gun.' However, he further stated that the stun gun wounds would have been lethal and he undermined Smit's theory by commenting, 'There's some danger in making a decision based on photographs without having talked to the people who did the autopsy and who saw the injuries.'

Smit stated that the Ramseys were loving parents with no motive for killing their child and no history of criminal or abusive behaviour. Their wealth and high profile made them a potential target for a kidnapper.

A couple of unexplained events added to the intruder theory. Unknown vehicles were reportedly parked outside the Ramseys' home near the time of the crime. In addition, JonBenet told a friend's mother that Santa Claus was going to pay her a 'special' visit after Christmas and that it was a secret.

Smit claimed the expertly constructed garrotte used on JonBenet indicated a sexual sadist and that JonBenet's vicious injuries occurred before her death and were not part of some postmortem staging. The ransom note was almost certainly written before JonBenet died by a brutal, calm and deliberate person.

A neighbour heard a piercing scream around midnight on the night of the murder and tests demonstrated that a scream could be heard more easily on the outside than further upstairs in the house. The next question is, how would an intruder be familiar with that unusual acoustic fact?

Neither Smit's nor Thomas's theory was conclusive; each had a number of details that militated against it. When the investigation stalled and ran out of steam, it seemed sensible to call in the FBI for help. This did not happen but the Boulder Police Department did accept an invitation from the FBI to present the case to the FBI's Child Abduction and Serial Killer Unit, CASKU, based in Quantico, Virginia.

The FBI View

Twenty CASKU agents, including hair and fibre experts, attended the August 1997 briefing where police investigators reviewed the autopsy findings and crime scene photos. CASKU agents noted that of the more than 1,700 murdered children they had studied since the early sixties, there was only one case in which the victim was female, under the age of twelve, had been murdered in her home by strangulation with sexual assault, and there was a ransom note present: JonBenet Ramsey. The agents told the Boulder investigators that, while it might be possible someone broke into the house on that day, it was not very probable.

The evidence presented to them by the Boulder police, and the totality of the case pointed in one direction: this was not the act of an intruder. Thomas wrote that the FBI team said, 'The crime did not fit an act of sex or revenge or one in which money was the motivation.'

They had never seen anything like the Ramsey ransom note. Kidnapping demands are usually terse: 'We have your kid. A million dollars. Will call you.' From a kidnapper's point of view, the fewer the words, the less the police have to go on. The FBI, according to Thomas, believed the note was written in the house after the murder, and indicated panic. Ransom notes are normally written prior to the crime and proofread, and not written by hand, in order to disguise the authors.

Thomas said that the FBI deemed the entire crime 'criminally unsophisticated', the child being left on the premises, the oddness of the $118,000 demand, and the concept of a ransom delivery where one would 'be scanned for electronic devices'. Kidnappers prefer isolated drops for the ransom delivery, not wanting a face to face meeting.

CASKU profilers also observed that placing JonBenet's body in the basement indicated involvement of a parent rather than an intruder. A parent would not want to place the body outside in the frigid night. They also stated that the ligatures 'indicated staging rather than control', and the garrotte was used from behind so the killer could avoid eye contact, typical of someone who cares for the victim. They had the gut feeling that 'no one intended to kill the child'.

Whoever killed JonBenet didn't fear getting caught. The FBI profilers conjectured that the crime 'was committed by someone who had a high degree of comfort inside the home'. The murderer spent a good deal of time with the victim, bashing her head, dragging her down two stories to the basement, wiping down her vaginal area, taping her mouth, tying up her wrists, garrotting her carefully, even lovingly placing a white blanket over her, calmly writing what the Boulder police called the War and Peace of ransom notes, and then placing that ransom note just where Patsy Ramsey would be most likely to find it when she came down the back stairs in the morning.

The process would after many months lead down the same blind alley that every other avenue had.

When the grand jury failed to bring an indictment and no special prosecutor was appointed, all hopes of solving the crime and bringing the perpetrator to trial faded.

The Ramseys revealed in their book that they were sure they would be indicted by the grand jury, so much so that they returned to Boulder before it ended its deliberations. This was to avoid being arrested in Atlanta and being forced to spend time in Fulton jail before being extradited to Colorado.

They had a morbid fear of being arrested and being handcuffed, they just wanted to be able to turn themselves in and post bond for immediate bail. It never happened, but that did not lift the cloud of suspicion that continued to hang over the parents of the victim because, of the two theories put forward, the one that pointed towards them was the strongest and the one of the intruder left open too many questions.

Despite the collective suspicion, polygraph tests could not find them lying, but these were rejected by prosecuting authorities as they were not carried out by the FBI. The Ramseys were never arrested, indicted or charged with the murder. There was another poignant milestone to this tragic saga when Patsy Ramsey died in June 2006.

One of the most high profile and controversial investigations in the US seemed to have ground to a halt with justice the loser.

Postscript

In August 2006 there was a bizarre and unexpected twist to this tragedy that already had reached and surpassed Greek proportions. A forty-one-year-old American teacher John Mark Karr, who four years earlier had fled the US after being served a charge of possessing child pornography, was arrested in Bangkok, Thailand. He had previously worked in Germany, Holland and South Korea.

At a press conference Karr stunned the assembled media by admitting responsibility for the murder of JonBenet Ramsey. He said that it was an accident and that he loved the girl, a statement that justifiably made the flesh creep on those present.

The statement that it was an accident was meaningless in support of his admission since it had long been established and completely accepted by the investigation that whoever was responsible had not intended to kill the six-year-old.

The first reports were sensational and with such a good story the media just ran with it without seriously questioning why any man would admit guilt for such a heinous crime under such circumstances. But once scrutiny became part of the reporting process it soon emerged that the confession posed more questions than answers to the solution of the decade-old crime.

First of all the genesis of the arrest, apart from the outstanding charges, came from an apparent obsession that Karr had with the killing of JonBenet. While he was a fugitive he started communicating with Michael Tracey, a Colorado University professor who had been involved in three documentaries on the murder and who was a supporter of the intruder theory and innocence of John and Patsy Ramsey.

Karr had also contacted Patsy Ramsey by e-mail before her death, sympathising on the death of her daughter but making no admissions.

Hundreds of e-mails were exchanged with Tracey but some of Karr's sentiments prompted the professor to alert the authorities and pass on the correspondence. In one, he asked the professor to go to the Ramseys' old house at Christmas and read out his crudely constructed ode of love:

> . . . JonBenet, my love, my life, I love you and shall forever love you. I pray that you can hear my voice calling to you from my darkness. We shall meet again and laugh together once more as we did in this life. If there is to be a life for me after this one, I pray it will be with you – together forever with you and other little girls who are forever gone from my life. This would be my heaven.

Whatever Tracey thought of Karr's obsession with the case or the unlikely scenario that he was involved in the killing, such a lewd expression of a paedophile's masturbatory fantasy of heaven with little girls would have been enough to prompt him to contact the authorities as no young girl could be safe from a man with such thoughts.

Karr, who had been charged with possession of child pornography, had married twice – both times to teenagers. At the age of nineteen he married Quientana Shotts, who was fourteen at the time. This marriage was annulled and a few years later he married a fifteen-year-old with whom he shared three children. His ex-wife Lara when contacted said that he had spent Christmas of 1996 with her and family in Alabama.

His father claimed that Karr had never been in Boulder, Colorado, and his half-brother supported both contentions.

But despite the now huge question mark over the veracity of Karr's confessions, reports quoted US law enforcement officials as believing that they had the man responsible. One told reporters that Karr knew graphic details about the crime that, he claimed, were only known to the medical examiner and a small group of investigators working on the case at the time.

This was patent nonsense, however, since Steve Thomas – one of those investigators – revealed in his book the postmortem findings, crime scene investigation and evidence collected in fine and graphic detail. All the details that needed to be known by Karr were already in the public domain.

And in the decade since, in all the documentaries, books, TV and media investigations, not once did the name of John Mark Karr come up in even the vaguest of connections. If this puny, weak-looking man, somewhat reminiscent of Lee Harvey Oswald, craved his instant piece of fame, he had clearly succeeded and in the most lurid of ways.

Karr obviously enjoyed the experience of being the centre of a media scrum and being self-cast in the role of a child killer. His statements, however, were vague beyond belief and there was, in fact, nothing linking him to the murder of JonBenet. In the end it was down to forensics, specifically DNA, to prove that this idle, nasty fantasist was typical of his kind – a nobody who wanted to become a somebody.

And that is exactly what happened. There was no match with the DNA found on the victim's body and Boulder authorities had no option but to drop all waiting charges. At the end of August 2006 Karr was hastily removed back to California to face the original charges of possession of child pornography.

Forensics had proved the former teacher as a self-serving liar who had wasted everyone's time for his small space in the spotlight.

The murder of child pageant queen, JonBenet Ramsey, a decade on, remains unsolved.

12

THE MURDER OF
RACHEL O'REILLY

There is increasing evidence that as crime scene investigation gets more efficient, criminals and killers are becoming more forensically aware and careful about leaving any trace of their presence at a crime scene. The proliferation of books about the subject, TV crime series such as *C.S.I.*, *Forensic Detectives* and *The F.B.I. Files*, as well as the vast amount of information available on the Internet, have provided criminals with knowledge that in previous generations was the sole preserve of the investigators.

Many killers now study the forensic implications of their actions in advance of the crimes. This practice has made the concept of the perfect crime a reality in too many cases and is particularly true of gangland murder where the success rate of conviction is practically nil. There are special circumstances here but killers outside that circle are also becoming adept at covering their tracks.

In some cases, the killers have not studied the subject of forensics sufficiently well, have slipped up and been caught but in others it is quite clear that the planning has been so thorough that even if the killer's identity is well known to the investigators there is not enough evidence to secure a conviction.

Killers who do not know their victims are less likely to commit the perfect murder, which, however, does not stop them trying. The killer who knows, has a relationship, a friendship or a family connection with the victim, and regular access to the victim's residence has a far better chance of success. The reason for this fact in the complicated scenario of murder is simple: evidence, which could convict a stranger or random killer, is of little or no value particularly if the victim is killed in the family home. Statistically, the vast majority of victims in this category have been killed by relatives, spouses or someone within the circle of friends.

Hair, fibre and fingerprints, vital links in the chain of murder evidence, can be rendered useless in a home crime scene, because the perpetrator, if close to the victim and having regular access to the home, would naturally leave such evidence to which nothing suspicious can be attached.

In this case what the perpetrator has most to be concerned with is the transfer of such evidence as blood and bodily matter from the victim at the time of the crime. However, time allowing, that simply entails destroying clothing worn at the scene and washing away any evidence transferred to the body.

Another advantage is that the crime scene is so familiar to the killer, a big help in the matter of destruction or concealment of evidence, or the arrangement or staging of the scene. A killing at the victim's residence is generally staged by the murderer to look like the work of an intruder, with robbery being utilised as a common motivation. In unusual cases the scene can be staged to look like a suicide.

Whatever the suggestion, the scene is arranged to deflect attention and point the finger of suspicion away from the perpetrator. A knowledge of forensics, the great ally of the investigator, can help the perpetrator literally to get away with murder. But if that knowledge is too little, it can, for the killer, prove to be a dangerous thing.

Like most mothers, Rachel O'Reilly's daily routine was centred around school time. Monday, October 4, 2004, was no different. At 8.40 that morning she left her house in Baldarragh about thirty kilometres from Dublin to drop off her four-year-old son, Luke, at Hedgestown Primary School. She then drove back over the M1 flyover to leave her two-year-old son, Adam, at a Montessori school outside Naul. This was to be the last time the two boys would ever see their mother alive.

Later that afternoon, staff at the Montessori grew worried when Rachel failed to collect Adam. It was most uncharacteristic of Rachel to be late and so, after an hour had passed, a member of staff phoned her land line before trying Rachel's mobile. There was no answer from either phone. With no success, the staff contacted her husband Joe who was at work in the Broadstone bus depot at the time.

Concerned though 'not overly panicked', Joe phoned Rachel's mother, Rose Cally, who immediately drove to

Rachel's house to see why her daughter had failed to pick up the two boys from school. Joe then phoned Rachel's neighbour – and best friend – Sarah Harmon. After collecting Adam, Sarah drove to the house, arriving just seconds after Rose. It was now about 1.30 p.m. Although Rose was indeed worried, seeing her daughter's car in the driveway provided some sense of relief. At least now she knew her daughter was safe at home. So she thought.

Rose noticed that the curtains on the window were drawn. This was unusual. The most natural thing for a mother to do in the morning is to open the curtains and let the natural light come in. To start the day with the outside world cut off would not have been Rachel's style and it was even more puzzling at this time of the day. Rose was gripped by an unnatural fear.

While Sarah waited in the car with Adam and her own two daughters, Rose entered the house through the unlocked back door with a sense of foreboding. Walking through the kitchen, she continued into the hallway where she encountered the terrifying sight of blood-stained walls. Horror coursed through every vein in her body.

Although she could barely dare to look, Rose's eyes were drawn to the open door of the nearby bedroom. There she was confronted with a sight that no parent should see: the dead body of her own child. Her beautiful daughter's battered body lay on the floor, covered in blood. Rose could only take the scene in briefly before running back outside to the car.

Rachel had been savagely bludgeoned to death with a blunt instrument, suffering numerous blows to the head.

Such was the ferociousness of the attack that her blood could be seen splattered across the bedroom walls. The once fit and healthy young woman was a bloody, battered mass, her golden hair matted with blood and brain tissue.

Rushing from the house, Rose told Sarah that Rachel had been in some sort of an accident and that they needed to call an ambulance as soon as possible. Though she knew her daughter was already dead, the brutal reality of the situation had not yet registered. Joe O'Reilly arrived minutes before the ambulance.

Recounting the moments of his return to the house, he said,

> Everything else – as you hear – was like an out-of-body experience. I just literally felt I was on the outside looking in on myself running into the house. Sarah was calling the emergency services when I got into the kitchen. She looked really, really upset as well, so I knew what I was about to see was going to be something bad but not as bad as what I actually saw.
>
> I went down to the bedroom and it was very bloody. It was very violent and instinct just kicked in, you know, to try and revive her . . . do some kind of CPR . . . something. As I checked for a sign of pulse, she felt like marble, very cold, very hard. I tried to move her and I couldn't . . . that was either because she was so stiff or the life had drained out of me.

Unfortunately by following this instinct to do something, an understandable reaction from any loving husband, Joe simply contaminated evidence such as hairs and fibres by touching the body. It might be argued that given the state of the scene and the horrific injuries obvious on the body that he should have known better, but sometimes emotion gets the better of judgement, especially when a loved one is the victim.

When the emergency services and the gardaí arrived it was quickly established that this was a clear case of murder. The thirty-year-old mother of two had been dragged into a desperate fight for her life after her killer attacked her in a vicious frenzy. 'There was a shocking level of violence prevalent in the attack, and the person who did it would have to be very motivated or be a complete psychopath,' said one investigator.

Investigators noticed that there were superficial indications that a robbery might have taken place. However, a robbery would not explain the levels of violence used against the victim. While the history of robbery has included cases where extreme violence and even murder has occurred, statistically it is relatively rare. The violence that Rachel O'Reilly was subjected to spoke clearly to detectives of a motive of which robbery had no part.

The murder was believed to have taken place shortly after 9.40 a.m. when Rachel returned home from her morning duties. She is believed to have been dead before the postman called to the house with a parcel containing cosmetics from Avon, which Rachel sold in the area. There was no answer when he rang the doorbell.

The family were full of grief and confusion. In the days that followed, more than two dozen bouquets of flowers were left outside Rachel's home by grieving neighbours and friends. Rose Callely later described the scene, recalling how Rachel's normally pale skin 'looked like marble'. She said, 'I knew to look at her before I knelt down that she was dead; she had such a horrific death.'

Rachel's mobile was taken by gardaí in an attempt to trace any contact she had with people outside of her family and friends in the weeks leading up to her death. The big mission was establishing the killer's motivation.

Rachel's father, Jim Callely, initially believed his daughter was the victim of a vicious stalker. He reckoned the attacker was watching Rachel and knew she would be alone in the house on the morning of her murder.

> None of this adds up. Rachel didn't have much
> and the crime scene was too neat and organised
> to be a burglary.

He also argued that the murder was not the work of a random stranger.

> Rachel was a very trusting person but she would
> never have let someone she didn't know into the
> house. It was as if someone just picked up a few
> things from a drawer and laid them out to make
> it look like a burglary.

Rose also agreed that the burglary scene looked 'contrived'. Furnishings and ornaments had been disturbed and an audit of the house contents revealed some missing items, including an old camcorder, small pieces of inexpensive jewellery and a couple of towels. None of these items were of significant value, yet they were taken while more than €1,000 was left sitting in a plastic container in the kitchen. The money in Rachel's purse was also left untouched. The gardaí admitted to being baffled by the prospect that Rachel may have been murdered by an intruder, stating that in over twenty years of house break-in's, a burglar has rarely killed anyone who disturbed them.

Despite their doubts, investigators went about checking the movements of known criminals, initially suspecting that if the motive was indeed that of robbery, then an inner-city gang linked with a spate of local break-ins could be the very perpetrators they were looking for. At this early stage it was important to follow up every lead and tease out every theory.

But as the break-in theory produced no leads, no tip-offs or information from the underworld, it was set aside, but properly and only after extensive inquiries.

The *Evening Herald* had been the first to react to the killing. They had run a story implying that Rachel had been beaten to death after she disturbed a burglar. Initially it was thought that the murder weapon might have been a hockey stick as it was known that Rachel played the game. Later, however, the tabloids proposed that Rachel had been beaten with a baseball bat when it emerged that she was one of the best softball players in the country. Neither theory was true.

In the bedroom where Rachel was murdered, there was a small set of weights. Gardaí later discovered that one of these barbells was missing. It was deduced that the killer used this heavy metal barbell to batter Rachel to death, smashing her skull over and over again as she lay dying on the bedroom floor. If a stranger had been involved, this would be considered a weapon of opportunity, but as the investigation progressed gardaí believed the killer knew that the barbells were present and had in fact carefully planned to give the impression that the murder weapon was just chanced upon.

The horrific death meted out to Rachel spoke either of a personal grudge fuelled by deep hatred or the work of a psychopath who enjoyed the control that the extreme violence gave and got sexual satisfaction from the pain and humiliation suffered by the victim.

While the psychopath can operate as a random killer, nothing at the scene of the crime suggested, particularly as a break-in was ruled out, that the murder was the act of a stranger. The monster that committed this heinous crime in fact clearly had a knowledge of not only the area and the routes of escape which allowed the minimum chance of being seen, but also, as would be proved, the house.

Detectives were inclined to believe that Rachel was killed in a murder that had been planned with military precision over a period of several months.

A forensic examination of the murder scene presented no signs of fingerprints of anyone in the Garda fingerprint database. This further enhanced the investigators' belief that the killer was known to Rachel, and that he may have been waiting for her to arrive home, or indeed that he had entered the house and was able to surprise her by striking her with the barbell.

An examination of the bath and shower unit unearthed samples of the victim's blood found in the plughole of the bath. This indicated that the killer had the poise and presence of mind to take a shower to wash the victim's blood from his body and remove vital DNA evidence after such a savage killing. Detectives were convinced that the perpetrator was familiar with the house and might well have carried out the murder while naked to obviate the necessity to dispose of blood-stained clothes – a rich source of evidence that might catch him. Whoever killed Rachel would have been completely covered in blood. It was sprayed all over the walls. Blood spatter analysis was later carried out by a British expert who established clearly that the killer could not have avoided a large amount of blood staining.

Immediately after the murder, gardaí began a meticulous search of the hedges, ditches and bushes around Baldarragh. Within a few days, they found the camcorder – which had the family name and address stamped on it – in a culvert underneath the road not far from the O'Reilly household. The murder weapon, believed to have been wrapped in a towel, was never found.

In their investigations, gardaí seized around 160 video tapes from CCTV cameras across north and west Dublin, attempting to map out the route taken by the killer's getaway car. However, the killer drove to and from the O'Reilly household along isolated back roads to avoid being captured on CCTV.

According to one investigator,

> The killer spent months planning this. We believe that he searched the area for CCTV cameras and followed a route where he would not be picked up on camera. Or at least he thinks he wasn't picked up on camera.

Detectives, who carefully pieced together the true story of what happened by combining the latest in forensic technology with the usual old-fashioned methods of enquiry, say that although the killer had everything planned down to the finest detail, he made one serious mistake which placed him near the murder scene. 'This evidence is incontrovertible and is 100% accurate.'

Detectives are convinced that the killer is deeply concerned, can't sleep at night, and is expecting to be arrested. 'We believe he is already preparing his answers but he is now terrified about what evidence we have in our possession.' In order to keep the killer confused, senior gardaí enforced a news blackout regarding the evidence they obtained.

On October 10 Rachel O'Reilly should have been celebrating her thirty-first birthday. Instead, her husband Joe and their two young sons were saying their last goodbyes before her body was removed from the family home the following day and taken to Holy Child Church in Whitehall, Co Dublin for the funeral service. Rachel was a member of the Renegades Softball Club and took part in the Irish World Record Softball events in 2002 and 2004. As a mark of respect, her team-mates attended the funeral wearing their team shirts.

Pale-faced and trembling, Joe O'Reilly stood at the altar and informed the congregation of his wish to address 'the person responsible' for the death of his beautiful 'Rach', his wife of just seven years. With tears welling in his eyes, he declared, 'Unlike you, she is at peace. Unlike you, she is sleeping. She forgives you, and I hope she gives me the strength someday to forgive you.' He then went on to describe Rachel's busy sporting life, and how she had travelled widely, fulfilling a number of her life goals by the age of thirty. These included getting married, having children, living in the country, having a sea view and having lots of friends. Said Joe, 'Mission accomplished Rachel, well done.' He then thanked her for her love and for making him laugh and added, 'See you on the other side. We all thank you. Bye for now.'

After the funeral, Joe was upfront about the investigation into his wife's brutal murder. He said at the time, 'I have nothing to hide – and I think the gardaí know that.' Joe also revealed he was carrying out his own enquiries and had offered gardaí several theories for the evil killing. He said he was personally investigating his wife's murder, even going as far as following up leads.

> Everyone, including myself, is a suspect until this is resolved. I was questioned in the same way everyone else was and statistically you know, eight out of ten times it's usually the husband or the boyfriend, or whatever. So maybe I'm not the number one suspect now, but at the start I was.

He told of how three gardaí had visited him one day, stating that they had 'some questions'. He recalled,

> They started off by asking if I had noticed anything missing, but then it was, 'Did you ever hit her?' I couldn't believe it, and they just explained it by saying, 'You do know this is a murder investigation?'

He firmly believed two intruders were involved in the murder, maintaining that Rachel was so fit she could have managed one attacker. She represented Ireland in softball, threw shot-put and discus for Leinster, studied the martial art of Tai Kwan-do, played hockey, lifted weights, enjoyed swimming and regularly went to the gym.

> She was very strong and would be well able to look after herself. If she suddenly came across an intruder she might have given as good as she got but then maybe another man came from another room and just hit her.

However his strongest belief was that Rachel knew her killer. His explanation was: 'I think they [the killers] knew her well enough. She might have asked them to the bedroom – something like that.' He then added, 'If someone tried to barge their way past her, then the blood would have been in the kitchen.' Joe also threw himself into an emotionally draining series of interviews in which he spoke over and over again of the pain he and Rachel's family were experiencing since the murder. He answered all questions – including those concerning the notion that Rachel was having an affair, something Joe has always strongly refuted.

> The biggest thing about Rach was her straightness. If she had met someone else, she was far too honest and brave not to have told me. Even if she was, what can I do about that now? Whatever happened that morning, there was someone in the house whom she knew. I don't believe it was an act of passion, but I think she was the victim of someone who knew her movements that morning.

Joe then concluded that he and Rachel were happily married.

Although at that time he was living with his mother in Dunleer in Co Louth, he spent some time at the house in Baldarragh sorting through Rachel's possessions and tidying up after forensic officers. On Friday, October 22, just two weeks after the death of his wife, Joe made an appearance on *The Late Late Show* accompanied by Rachel's mother, Rose.

In the audience was Rachel's father Jim, her sister Ann and her close friend and neighbour, Sarah Harmon. Composed to the point where he appeared almost emotionless, Joe shared with the nation everything from the time he proposed to Rachel on top of the Eiffel Tower in 1994 to the day he saw her bloodied body lying dead on their bedroom floor. Right throughout the interview, Joe maintained his belief that Rachel's death was not as a result of a botched burglary, but that she was killed because her attacker was someone she knew.

He said he believed that Rachel was hit a number of times when she was on the ground and that her killer made sure she was dead so that she could not identify him. He explained,

> Rachel was not stupid. If she walked in on a burglary, she'd have known. She would have walked straight out of the house and called someone. Nothing justifies the violence and the excess of what happened. It just doesn't fit. Why kill her? We feel it's because she could identify the person.

The 6ft 5in Dubliner also explained that on the morning his wife was murdered, he had left the house at 6.30 a.m. to go to a gym on the Naas Road before travelling to his workplace in the Bluebell Industrial Estate. He then said he went to the Broadstone bus depot where he went about his work inspecting advertisement boards on Dublin buses.

Sarah Harmon, defeated by grief, was just about able to

read a poem she had written for Rachel. The dead woman's sister was also in tears and clung to her father's hand for support.

During that same month, a reconstruction of Rachel's murder was broadcast on RTÉ's *Crimecall*. At the end of the segment, Joe O'Reilly appeared briefly to ask viewers to report anything they might have seen, no matter how small. He also pleaded with them to remember that two young boys had been robbed of their mother and that Rachel's parents had lost a daughter. He later informed a Sunday tabloid of his discomfort in watching the re-enactment. 'I'm not doing too good,' he explained. 'I found that reconstruction incredibly hard to watch. My heart was just in my mouth.'

Joe has also spoken of his attempts in trying to explain the situation to his eldest son Luke. He told the four-year-old that his mummy had gone to heaven, but he wasn't sure how much he understood.

> The boys went back to school and some of the kids must have said something because he was asking what happened. I said she fell and hurt her head. Being four, he asked if I put a plaster on and I said I did. I don't think it will really sink in until we move back into the house. I know Rachel is not coming back but I really can't accept that she's gone. It's something you see on TV and does not happen to people. I will always regret not being able to say goodbye.

With the end of October approaching, he suddenly began to absorb the reality of life without his wife.

> It really hit me. It was Adam's third birthday and reading all the cards and not having Rachel there . . . it was so hard. I've been a basket case ever since to tell you the truth.

The O'Reillys had been planning to throw a Halloween party for their son's birthday. At the time of her death, Rachel was organising a magician as a surprise for young Adam. Instead, Joe brought his two boys and ten friends to a Leisureplex in Coolock. 'We're all absolutely dreading Christmas,' he said.

Joe's face soon found its way onto the front of each tabloid when rumours emerged that he was the one who had been having the affair. He argued,

> There is no other woman in my life and I have never had an affair – absolutely and definitely not. I was asked that question by the gardaí, and I told them 'absolutely not'.

O'Reilly revealed that he had been looking at everyone as a potential suspect.

> I have given the names of people to the gardaí and I will gladly apologise to them when the murderer is found, but until then, if I have to make enemies, I will.

He has also given the name of a person who was known to

both Rachel and himself.

> We have known this person for some time, and
> he is quite odd. We are not overly friendly with
> him and he may have been in the house that
> morning.

The O'Reillys had only recently moved to the Naul in order
to escape the busy city life of the capital. Even though
Baldarragh was only thirty kilometres away from Dublin city
centre, it might as well have been located at the very heart of
Connemara such was the tranquil beauty of its surroundings.

In an interview with a Sunday newspaper, Joe clutched
Rachel's photograph and spoke candidly about the day their
idyllic haven was shattered to smithereens.

> I will never get over her death. We had
> everything going for us. We only moved into our
> new home last year. We thought we had it all.
> We were in this great house, we had our two
> kids and we were just getting ready to enjoy life
> again because it can be pretty tough with two
> small children.

In the year the family had lived in the area, they managed to
forge close ties with the community, with Rachel actively
lending her support to an anti-dump group that was opposing
a proposed new landfill site. It was recalled by many how she
had thrown herself into the life of the local community in the
eighteen months since she and her husband had moved from

Dublin. Though several close friends described Rachel as being 'a lovely, bubbly young woman devoted to her family', interestingly enough they had also observed her as being 'unhappy with personal problems' in the weeks leading up to her death. According to one friend,

> Rachel was a very straight talker and you always knew if there was something on her mind. There was something definitely bothering her in the last few months. Unlike her, she didn't say what it was, but I knew from the way she was behaving that she was worried about something.

Police examined the alibis of everyone known to Rachel. Although each individual appeared to have an adequate explanation as to their whereabouts for that morning, two particular statements – one made by a man who knew Rachel and the other by his associate – came under close scrutiny as new evidence was found, which contradicted their accounts. Towards the very end of October, details emerged to support speculations that investigating officers had whittled their suspect list down to one main individual. Officers then confirmed that the suspect was a married man who had extra-marital relationships. One senior detective said at the time,

> The man who murdered Rachel is a psychopath.
> He is a highly dangerous man capable of extreme violence. He will not get away with this horrendous crime.

Gardaí were not satisfied with the alibi of the prime suspect. If they could connect him to the scene of the crime, it would demolish his alibi and significantly increase the prospects of him being charged. News of a possible breakthrough came a month to the day after Rachel was murdered. Detectives traced CCTV footage that they believed would discredit the suspect's alibi. Technical experts enhanced several pieces of the CCTV footage in order to confirm that the person on the video was the actual suspect. The footage was taken from CCTV cameras based in north Dublin on the route between the city and Rachel's home in the Naul.

On November 13, as gardaí prepared to arrest their prime suspect, husband Joe led mourners at a mass held to remember his wife. Outside Whitehall church, Joe embraced Rachel's mother, Rose, as he sympathised with members of her family. The mass was the first time Joe had seen many of Rachel's friends, colleagues and extended friends since her funeral. Although he appeared upbeat, friends claimed he was just about holding himself together. By this stage, Joe had ceased all contact with the media and had stopped making appeals for information on his wife's murder. Even though over a month had passed, O'Reilly, along with his two sons, Adam and Luke, was still living with his mother.

Also on November 13 detectives confirmed they were finished with their investigations, stating they had identified the killer three weeks earlier using technical evidence supplied by Garda headquarters. They were now satisfied that Rachel knew her killer and that he was acting alone.

Gardaí also revealed they had deliberately leaked false information to the media to confuse their prime suspect.

Although friends of the prime suspect provided officers with alibis, gardaí did not believe they were involved in the brutal murder, maintaining that these friends just could not bring themselves to believe the prime suspect would be capable of such violence. One 'alibi-provider' is a friend of the suspect, while the other is his secret mistress. The prime suspect and his mistress had been in a relationship for almost two years. She was interviewed by gardaí and said she met the suspect on the morning of the murder. Said one source to a newspaper,

> His girlfriend is trying to convince herself that he is innocent and would not be capable of hurting anyone. When she was interviewed, she simply confirmed that she knew the suspect and that she met with him on the morning of the murder. But we know parts of her story are not true. She is being evasive out of loyalty to the suspect. She would think differently if she saw how Rachel died, however this does not make her an accessory to the murder.

On Wednesday November 17, Joe O'Reilly was arrested for questioning in connection with his wife's murder. He was arrested at his home in the Naul and questioned under Section 4 of the Criminal Justice Act. He was held for almost the maximum of twelve hours before being released. As the weapon used in the murder was not a firearm, gardaí had to depend on the provisions of the act to hold him. It meant that they could only detain him for six hours which they were allowed to extend by a further six hours on the instruction of a chief superintendent. If Rachel had been shot, gardaí would have been allowed to detain any suspect for up to three days under the Offences Against the State Act.

Late on Wednesday night Joe O'Reilly was released without charge. Joe has always strenuously denied any involvement in the murder, and refused to comment as he left the station, watched by a crowd of up to fifty people who had gathered outside. He was then driven away in a Fiat Punto by two men.

A man, originally from Finglas but now living in Co Kildare, and a woman, were arrested the day before, Tuesday 16, on suspicion of withholding information about the circumstances leading up to Rachel's murder. They were released without charge.

The next time Joe O'Reilly's name made it into the papers was when a tabloid photographer snapped him 'treating the children to a Christmas break', visiting an ambulance depot in Derry. Joe and his two kids spent the Christmas period in Northern Ireland with his younger brother, who works as an ambulance driver at the local Altnagelvin ambulance station. Sources say Joe, understandably, wanted to escape the controversy and furore surrounding his wife's murder. During the visit, he and his sons attended a children's Christmas party put on by the staff at the station. Said one source to a newspaper, 'Joe was in good spirits considering all that happened to him last year.'

O'Reilly has distanced himself from his wife's family and friends since he was arrested. He is no longer on speaking terms with some of Rachel's close friends. With the pressure fast piling on, Joe O'Reilly declined through his solicitor, Peter Mullan, to speak again to the media. However, Joe's mother, Anne O'Reilly, insists her son is innocent.

> If I thought for a second that he had anything to do with Rachel's death, I would disown him. He would not be allowed under my roof. Anyone who knows Joe and the relationship he had with Rachel will know he positively had no involvement in the murder. People will say I am his mother and naturally I will stick by him. That's what mothers do, they will say. But no one knows Joe better than me. I reared him and brought him up. I know what I am talking about. As far as I'm concerned, he has been in a state of very deep shock since day one. The truth of the matter is that he is in no fit state to talk to anyone. He has been the focus of such dreadful attention that he simply cannot take any more. He is a good and kind-natured son, and it is not in his character to be violent to anyone.

Joe's mother told of how her family's lives had been torn asunder by Rachel's death. Anne, who works with children with learning disabilities, complained that the pressures on the family were now so great that she had been unable to go to her place of work in recent times.

So far, Rachel's family have said very little, if anything at all, about Joe O'Reilly. However it is known that the Callely family and Joe O'Reilly had fallen out long before he was announced as a suspect. Within days of the brutal killing, relations were said to be 'frosty' between Rachel's parents and her husband. Today, Rachel's family are 'completely disgusted and outraged' at the amount of media hype over the case. An anonymous source told one Sunday newspaper, 'They don't want anything to damage the integrity of their lovely Rachel and they don't want anything that will endanger the Garda enquiry into her death.'

Rose later told the same newspaper that the whole scenario was 'a nightmare, and I am afraid to go to sleep at night for what I might dream.'

In March 2005 Rachel's husband and a woman were again arrested and taken in for questioning by the investigation team and both were released later without charge.

In the interim, the brutal, merciless slaying of a young mother, daughter, wife and a woman with a fine past and a promising future goes unsolved and unpunished.

The murder weapon has never been recovered. Objects including CCTV footage have been sent to England for further tests and analysis.

Recently, gardaí investigating the murder sent a file to the Director of Public Prosecution after gathering evidence over a twenty-one-month period. The file, which extends to four volumes, is based almost wholly on circumstantial evidence, analysis of mobile phones and forensic detail. It is an illustration of the problems of evidence and proof that arise when a victim is murdered in his or her own home.

EPILOGUE:
THE SCOURGE
OF THE KILLER

There are many cases worldwide which are instructive of how crime scene investigation and forensic science track down and convict killers. Some will escape the net of investigation but the majority, through the commitment and dedication of the forces of law, end up spending a long time behind bars – despite the iniquities of a justice system which places huge pressure on the police and requires the allocation of enormous resources to them.

The perpetrators may try to hide their crime or attempt to lie their way out, the justice system may relegate the victim to a secondary position in court, but forensics will, in the vast majority of cases, prove to be the victim's greatest ally and the scourge of the killer.

Rachel Kiely decided to take the dogs for a walk in Ballincollig, a quiet village that is now a suburb of Cork city. Later on that evening the pretty twenty-two-year-old planned to attend a Bible study meeting of the Jehovah's Witness congregation so the walk would not be that long and she would take it at a brisk pace. The light at that time of the year was fading fast, but Rachel had nothing to fear from the dark;

she had taken the walk many times and she lived in a peaceful neighbourhood with no history of trouble or violence. A beautician by trade, she took her religion very seriously and that faith gave her both security and comfort in the face of life's difficulties. Her family who also belonged to the Jehovah's Witness religious group were very supportive of Rachel's desire to spread the word of the Gospel and 'the truth' as it was referred to by the faithful.

Rachel was surrounded by the love of her family and strengthened by her belief. She was young, idealistic and her life stretched before her with infinite possibilities. There was nothing to fear as she set out to take that familiar route with her dogs along a popular pathway which followed the course of the River Lee past Ballincollig.

About an hour after she left the dogs returned to the family home. There was no sign of Rachel and her mother Rose immediately became concerned. The family organised a search with the help of neighbours. They encountered a local sixteen-year old youth Ian Horgan who told them that he had not seen the missing young woman. It was a lie.

Less than two hours later a group – including her family – discovered her body in a clump of bushes behind a derelict house. She was lying in the foetal position. The gardaí were called and an investigation team went to the scene. The crime scene was photographed and shot on video tape.

The State Pathologist, Dr Harbison, who arrived the next day, noted that the victim was lying in a 'coiled up position' in an overgrown thicket. His examination of the surroundings indicated that Rachel had fled into the deep undergrowth as if she was trying to get away from an attacker, but the thickness of the bushes at that point had literally trapped her. She could not escape whoever was pursuing her. The pathologist also noticed an area of swelling and bruising on the left side of the neck. This indicated that the victim had experienced difficulty breathing, possibly due to strangulation.

There was bruising to her knees and right thigh suggesting that force was exerted on the inside of both knees to force them apart, immediately suggesting that Rachel had been raped. This was confirmed later by the postmortem at Cork University Hospital when vaginal swabs revealed the presence of semen. Rachel Kiely had been viciously raped and strangled.

The technical team also collected a number of fibres from the jacket of the dead woman which appeared to originate from another source. A red woollen hat with an Arsenal logo which had been found close to Ian Horgan's motorbike and was subsequently established as belonging to him was also examined. As part of the ensuing investigation DNA samples were taken from a number of men in the area including Ian Horgan.

The DNA profile of the semen taken from Rachel's body matched the profile of the saliva and hair samples taken from Horgan. He was subsequently arrested, questioned and clothes belonging to him taken and sent to the state laboratory for forensic examination. There Dr Maureen

Smith compared fibres taken from Rachel's fleece jacket with the clothing taken by the investigation team. She found that four green acrylic fibres, two blue acrylic fibres and two brown fibres on the fleece matched fibres from Horgan's jumper.

She also examined the red woollen hat and found that four red acrylic fibres from the hat were on the victim's fleece. Fibres from Horgan's jumper were also found on the hat.

Although Rachel Kiely had been brutally silenced, forensic evidence spoke for her, inextricably linking Horgan to the victim and therefore to the murder. On November 10, 2000, Horgan was charged with sexual assault and murder at a special sitting of the Cork District Court. Despite the evidence the accused vehemently denied the charges. His denial fell on deaf ears and in the Central Criminal Court in 2002 following a seven-week trial he was convicted of the rape and murder of Rachel Kiely.

This verdict was reduced to manslaughter and rape on appeal, the implication being that Horgan had not intended to kill Rachel Kiely. If his prime motivation was rape then why did he strangle the victim and attempt to conceal the body? It was clear from the evidence at the crime scene that after the rape the victim attempted to escape like a frightened animal from a predator and was hunted into the cul de sac created by the thick bushes. Her life was then mercilessly snuffed out by Horgan, the effect being to prevent a victim of rape from identifying her attacker. Was this really a spur of the moment action which might qualify for the category of manslaughter?

Not one whit of forensic evidence was capable of supporting that contention.

While Rachel's family were justifiably upset by the result of the appeal they can be grimly satisfied with the knowledge that this unsupported legal semantic cannot diminish the fact that their daughter suffered the fate that Horgan was originally convicted for. The simple fact is that the law can be an ass and a perpetrator may be in a permanent state of self-serving denial, but forensic science does not lie.

A classical example which proved this tenet happened in Leicestershire, England in the 1980s. In 1983 in the small town of Narborough a fifteen-year-old schoolgirl was found raped and murdered. A semen sample taken from Lynda Mann's body was found to belong to a person with type A blood group and enzyme profile. This matches ten percent of the adult male population, such a large group that conviction in court of a suspect would have proved very difficult, being just three years before the discovery of DNA profiling. The murder hunt was wound down for lack of evidence and a chief suspect.

Three years later Dawn Ashworth, also fifteen, was found strangled and sexually assaulted in the same town. The investigation team were convinced that the same person was responsible for both murders, but proving it was another matter. Semen samples taken from Dawn's body matched in blood type those from the first victim.

The prime suspect was a local boy. Under questioning, he

revealed details of the crime scene where Dawn was found which police felt only the perpetrator could know. He confessed, but the suspect denied being involved in Lynda's murder.

Investigators felt that something did not add up and, convinced that the same man (not the suspect) had committed both crimes, sought the help of Professor Alec Jeffreys of Leicester University who had just developed a technique for creating DNA profiles. He had, along with colleagues Dr Peter Gill and Dr Dave Werrett of the Forensic Science Service (FSS), first published a paper on the application of DNA profiling to forensic science. In 1985 they demonstrated that DNA could be extracted from stains at a crime scene.

The key to the process was an extraction method to separate sperm from vaginal cells. Using this method, Professor Jeffreys compared semen samples from both murders with a blood sample from the suspect. It conclusively proved that both victims were killed by the same man. The suspect was eliminated as a result of this forensic evidence.

Investigators then undertook the first ever DNA screening. All male adults in three nearby villages were asked to volunteer blood and saliva samples. The field was narrowed down to the 10% of men who had blood type A. The killer almost escaped detection by getting a friend to impersonate him in the testing process but colleagues overheard him telling what he did.

A local baker Colin Pitchfork was arrested. His semen

matched that taken from both murder victims and in 1988 he was sentenced to life for the murders.

Again in England, the killer of sixteen-year-old Leanne Tiernan was tracked down through analysis of fibres, mitochondrial DNA testing, and even dog DNA. West Yorkshire police launched a murder investigation following the discovery of Leanne's badly decomposed body in August 2001, nine months after she went missing after a shopping trip. Fingerprints, DNA and clothing identified the body as that of the missing Leeds teenager. Forensic scientists from the FSS were drafted in to the investigation and eventually linked the suspect to the crime.

Leanne's body was discovered in a duvet cover and a number of green plastic refuse sacks which were tied with twine. Her head was covered by a black plastic bag, which was held in place by a dog collar. A scarf and plastic cable tie had been tied around her neck, and cable ties bound together her wrists. Forensic scientists concentrated on building up a profile of the murderer. This work, combined with police investigation relating to the supplier of the dog collar and cable ties, ultimately led to a man by the name of John Taylor.

They examined the knitted scarf found around Leanne's neck and discovered hairs caught in the knot. Conventional DNA tests on the hair roots failed but using mitochondrial tests a profile was obtained from the minute amounts of DNA inside the hair shaft. It matched Taylor. The twine was examined and it was discovered that it had an unusual composition. Examination of twine found at Taylor's house found an exact match. It was traced to a manufacturer in Devon who sold it for rabbit netting. Only one small one-off batch was ever made.

Red nylon carpet fibres were recovered from Leanne's jumper and when these were examined they were discovered to be very distinctive, due to the unusual way in which the fibre had been dyed. Taylor had a red carpet which he had tried to burn. Examination provided another match.

Dog hairs had been found on the body and a forensic scientist took a sample to a Texan university which had provided DNA profiling for dogs, principally for pedigree research. A partial DNA profile of the dog was obtained but as the suspect's dog had died this did not help the case.

But there was more than enough evidence to link the prime suspect. When confronted, Taylor admitted his involvement and got two life sentences for kidnap and murder at Leeds Crown Court in July 2002.

Deborah Robinson a native of Belfast came to Dublin on a blind date in early September of 1980. The date did not go to plan so she decided to return to Belfast on a bus earlier than she had anticipated. She never made it home. Two days later on September 8 her body was found in a ditch in Kildare. She had been raped and strangled. An examination of the crime scene uncovered some vital fibre evidence.

Pieces of thread, all roughly the same size and cleanly cut at either end, were found in large amounts on the body.

Investigators immediately surmised that because of the rural location of the crime scene this evidence had been deposited on the body in a different place. It was clear that Deborah had been murdered somewhere else and her body transported and dumped in the ditch.

Discovering the origin of the fibres would lead detectives to the real crime scene and closer to the killer who had attempted to distance himself and conceal his connection to the crime by moving the body. The focus of the investigation was tracking the trail left by this evidence.

Investigators began to collect samples from every garment factory in the Kildare, Meath and Dublin areas. Fibres from each sample were compared to those taken from the body. It was a painstaking and frustrating process. It took one month short of a year for a match to be found. This came from a factory off Arran Quay in Dublin. Blood samples were taken from all twelve men working there to make a comparison with the semen sample taken from the woman's body.

The discovery of DNA fingerprinting was still a few years away but blood typing, despite its limitations, did succeed in narrowing the hunt down to three of the male workers. One of these, another Belfast native Richard O'Hara became the prime suspect. He had a previous criminal history for assault and theft. He had quit his job four days after the murder.

O'Hara was brought in for questioning and when confronted with the fact that his blood matched the semen sample, he confessed to killing Deborah who just happened to be in the wrong place at the wrong time. He had seen her standing at a bus stop and had come out of the factory to engage her in conversation. The fact that he was from Belfast put the unsuspecting victim at her ease. He offered Deborah a lift and she accepted. Purporting to bring her to his van, he lured her into the then empty factory where he brutally raped and murdered her.

From the floor near the cutting tables, fibres attached to the victim's clothes. O'Hara dragged the body along the floor collecting more fibre evidence, brought it to the van and later dumped it in the ditch. O'Hara had assumed that nothing could connect him to the crime, there was no witness and nothing to challenge his alibi. But the fibre evidence and blood sample were sufficient proof to ensure justice and a life sentence for the killer.

None of us knows what is waiting around the next corner. Some might say why bother thinking about it as fate will have its way. That may well be true but the history of murder, most particularly in the past decade in Ireland, has proved one fact beyond all doubt: a woman, no matter in what part of the country, is constantly at risk from physical assault, rape and murder. There is only one lesson to be learnt – vigilance should be maintained at all times. There have been too many dreadful cases of the stalker and the female victim.

As the murder of Dublin-based civil servant Marilyn Rynn illustrates, once there is killing in the mind of a perpetrator, all it needs is a chance encounter to provide the opportunity. The motive is already there, all that is required is the victim.

Epilogue: The Scourge of the Killer

It was a time for warmth, comfort, goodwill, love and celebration, an aspiration for most at Christmas time. But in the evil recesses of the mind of one man there was instead an overwhelming lust to rape and kill. It did not matter that he had a job and a family, responsibility and security, he was prepared to risk all to satisfy a compulsion. The urge was to control, torture, humiliate and kill an innocent woman.

Christmas did not matter, his family did not matter, his workmates and friends were distant shadows. Not only had he rehearsed the killing scenario in his fantasy world, he had studied the forensic implications of rape on the Internet. He knew that semen was a genetic fingerprint that would inextricably link him to the victim.

But he also learned that the sample can deteriorate within the victim's body over a relatively short period. If the body could be concealed successfully, then quite quickly he could escape the DNA net. It would depend on the circumstances of the encounter. If he was not caught then that would provide an incentive to satisfy the compulsion again and again. Such an evil urge can take a long time to grow and rarely ever goes away.

On the night of December 22, 1995, forty-one-year-old Marilyn Rynn who worked at the National Roads Authority section in Ballsbridge attended the office party at the Old Sheiling Hotel in Raheny. At 2 a.m she left the hotel and took a taxi into O'Connell Street where she met some work friends in Eddie Rockets diner. About an hour later she crossed O'Connell Bridge and got a Nitelink bus which left her near her home in Blanchardstown where she lived. Although she had plenty of cash, she could have been waiting for hours for a taxi at that time of the year. Besides she had no reason to fear the walk from the bus stop to her home, even though it involved a short cut along the Tolka Valley park and through a dark and thickly wooded area. She had no idea that she was walking straight into the radar of a compulsive man. It was the chance encounter that he had rehearsed so many times in his fantasy world.

Marilyn, a content, ordered and happy woman never made it home and never lived to spend Christmas with her beloved family. Some days later her worried family reported her missing. Her body was not found until a search was undertaken of the wooded area on January 6. It looked like time was on the side of the killer, any DNA evidence could well have deteriorated. Had it been summer that might well have been the outcome but it was an extremely cold and dry period. The semen sample recovered from the victim's body was well preserved by the low temperatures.

The investigation that followed involved a vast trawl through suspect lists. Gardaí took more than 2,000 statements and 354 blood samples for DNA testing. During the house-to-house enquiries in the immediate follow up to the discovery of the body, a local man by the name of David Lawler, thirty-one years of age, was interviewed. He admitted that he had walked home from his own office party on the night of December 22 and was in the vicinity in the early hours of the following morning.

At first he did not fit the profile of a murderer. The long-haired bearded technician had a steady job, wife and six-year-old son. One of five children, he had joined Telecom Éireann as a bright school-leaver from Baltinglass, Co Wicklow. He worked installing phone and computer modem lines and was a keen user of the Internet. Outward appearances, however, often superficially disguise the mind of a killer.

In February 1996 he voluntarily gave a blood sample to the investigating team. Apparently he had nothing to hide. The following July results came back from the laboratory and gardaí found a match between the semen sample and Lawler's blood. On August 6 he was arrested and charged with the murder. Later he admitted that he had been walking behind the victim in the wooded area and on a spontaneous impulse had attacked her. He raped her and strangled her with his hands. He hid her body in thick brambles, leaving her clothes and handbag nearby.

He pleaded guilty and was subsequently sentenced to life imprisonment. His little knowledge of forensic science proved a dangerous thing and rebounded on him. It was that science and dogged police work that proved his undoing. Justice was served very well by the crime scene investigation, subsequent police work and the elements, which David Lawler never put into the equation – the cold weather.

BIBLIOGRAPHY

Kenneth Anger, *Hollywood Babylon,* Stonehill Publishing (1975)

Steve Hodel, *Black Dahlia Avenger*, Perennial (2004)

John Gilmore, *Severed*, Granta Books (2004)

Janice Knowlton, *Daddy was the Black Dahlia Killer*, Pocket Books (1995)

James Ellroy, *The Black Dahlia*, Mysterious Press (1987)

James Ellroy, *L.A. Confidential*, Arrow Books (2005)

Lawrence Schiller, *Perfect Murder, Perfect Town*, Harper Paperbacks (1999)

Colin Beavan, *Fingerprints: Murder and the Race to Uncover the Science of Identity*, Fourth Estate (2002)

Dr Michael Baden and Marion Roach, *Dead Reckoning: The New Science of Catching Killers*, Arrow Books (2001)

Samantha Weinberg, *Pointing from the Grave: A True Story of Murder and DNA*, Hamish Hamilton (2003)

N.E. Genge, *The Forensic Casebook: The Science of Crime Scene Investigation*, Ebury (2004)

Colin Evans, *The Casebook of Forensic Detection: How Science Solved 100 of the World's Most Baffling Crimes*, John Wiley & Sons, Canada (1998)

Ronald R. Thomas, *Detective Fiction and the Rise of Forensic Science*, Cambridge University Press (1999)

Hugh Miller, *Forensic Fingerprints: Remarkable Real-Life Murder Cases Solved by Forensic Detection*, Headline, London (1998)

John Hunter, *Studies in Crime: Introduction to Forensic Archaeology*, Routledge, London (1997)

Donna M. Jackson, *The Bone Detectives: How Forensic Anthropologists Solve Crimes and Uncover the Mysteries of the Dead*, Little Brown (2001)

Niamh O'Connor, *Cracking Crime, Jim Donovan – Forensic Detective*, The O'Brien Press (2001)

Stephen Rae, *Guilty: Violent Crimes in Ireland*, Blackwater Press (2002)

Other Sources

The Irish Times; Irish Independent; Irish Examiner; Sunday Independent; BBC; RTÉ; Court TV; *The Forensic Detectives*, Discovery Channel; *The FBI Files*, Discovery Channel; Crown Forensic Service; Crime Library, Google search sites.

Frozen Blood

Michael Sheridan

Murder is an unspeakable horror but even more sickening depths are reached by serial and psycho killers.

Best-selling author Michael Sheridan describes a distinct and brutal pattern of killing women which has emerged in Ireland, one used by psycho sex killers.

To powerful and disturbing effect, *Frozen Blood* examines the circumstances surrounding the murder and disappearance of several women. Young women such as Phyllis Murphy, who was raped and viciously killed, and Raonaid Murray, who was brutally attacked with a six-inch kitchen knife, murdered by men who have no inhibitions or feelings of remorse.

Why does an innocent child turn into a depraved killer? What are the common denominators among the tiny percentage of people who savagely kill? Why do they do what they do? Tracing the horrifying phenomenon of psychotic sex killers, *Frozen Blood* provides terrifying profiles of killers active in Ireland.

Tears of Blood

Michael Sheridan

Murder and unlawful killing are now so common in Ireland that they no longer command headline attention. A daily perusal of the papers will provide dreadful details of killings. These details, the cases and the trials are publicly aired and then the media move on to the next story. But as best-selling author Michael Sheridan discovers, the effects of murder and killing are far-reaching for the families and relatives of the victims.

Through interviews with the families left behind and by researching inquest files and postmortem reports, the author reconstructs the crimes and exposes the horrific acts of merciless killers such as Noel Hogan, the Ian Huntley of Ireland; Peter Whelan; Anthony Kiely and Thomas Murray. Killers and murderers constantly lie about the crime; the facts do not.

Chronicling the devastating effects on the families of the victims, who include Lorraine O'Connor, Nichola Sweeney, Bernadette Connolly and Nancy Nolan, *Tears of Blood* provides a unique and heart-rending insight into the aftermath of murder.

Irish Crimes of Passion

Liam Collins

**Crime is perilous.
Crime and passion are a
lethal cocktail.**

Picture the beautiful temptress
who buys her own grave, then
lures her lover to a dramatic
death scene in her bedroom . . .

. . . the husband who goes
through his wife's mobile
phone messages and unleashes a
rage that not only leads to her murder but wipes out an entire
family . . .

. . . or the coward brooding in a love triangle who hires
a ruthless killer to murder his pregnant wife.

They are all here in the hidden Ireland, where ordinary men
and women suddenly get caught up in that deadly moment when
crime and passion collide – with fatal consequences.

Liam Collins investigates these tragic cases where love, lust,
desire and jealousy twist and contort in a spiral of madness.

**'. . . captures the dark underbelly of Irish society
where violence and lust lurk just below the surface
and erupt with terrible consequences . . .'
PAUL WILLIAMS, crime writer**

ORDER FORM

Please fill in your details below

Please send me __ copies of Frozen Blood @ €9·99 each
__ copies of Tears of Blood @ €11·95 each
__ copies of Irish Crimes of Passion @ €11·95 each

I enclose cheque ☐ postal order ☐
credit card ☐☐☐☐☐☐☐☐☐☐☐☐☐☐☐☐☐☐☐
Expiry date ☐☐ ☐☐ Mastercard ☐ Visa ☐
to the value of € _____

Name: _____

Address: _____

_____

Tel: _____

Email: _____

Please return to: **MENTOR BOOKS,**
43 Furze Road, Sandyford Ind. Est, Dublin 18

Tel: (01) 2952112/3   Fax: (01) 2952114
email: admin@mentorbooks.ie
website: www.mentorbooks.ie